HOW TO
FORAGE FOR
WILD FOODS
without dying

T0384141

HOW TO
FORAGE FOR
WILD FOODS
without dying

An Absolute Beginner's Guide to
IDENTIFYING 40 EDIBLE
WILD PLANTS

ELLEN ZACHOS

Storey Publishing

The mission of Storey Publishing is to serve our customers by
publishing practical information that encourages
personal independence in harmony with the environment.

Edited by Carleen Madigan and Sarah Slattery
Art direction and book design by Erin Dawson
Text production by Liseann Karandisecky and Jennifer Jepson Smith
Cover photography by © Ellen Zachos, IBC; © Ernie Janes/Alamy Stock Photo, back t.l.; © Flower_Garden/
Shutterstock.com, back b.r.; © fotomarekka/Shutterstock.com, back m.r.; © IhorM/Shutterstock.com, back b.l.;
© Irina Borsuchenko/Shutterstock.com, back m.l.; © Kabar/Shutterstock.com, back t.r.; © krblokhin/iStock.
com, IFC; © William Berry/Alamy Stock Photo, front
Interior photography credits appear on page 253

This book is intended as an educational refer-
ence, and the information in this book is true
and complete to the best of our knowledge. All
recommendations are made without guarantee
on the part of the author or publisher, and the
author and publisher disclaim any liability in
connection with the use of this information. In
particular, eating wild plants is inherently risky.
Plants can be easily mistaken, and individuals vary
in their physiological reactions to plants that are
touched or consumed. Also, pregnancy, allergies,
or health conditions can all affect whether the
information or recommendations in this book
are appropriate for you. If you have questions,
you should consult with your doctor before you
begin a new routine or eat plants gathered in the
wild. Any reader who forages for wild foods and
chooses to ingest them does so at his or her own
risk; without a 100% positive identification, no
wild foods should ever be consumed. Consulting
with an expert forager, who can identify the wild
foods in person, is recommended.

The information in this book is true and complete to
the best of our knowledge. All recommendations are
made without guarantee on the part of the author
or Storey Publishing. The author and publisher disclaim any liability in connection with the use of this
information.

The publisher is not responsible for websites (or
their content) that are not owned by the publisher.

Storey books may be purchased in bulk for business,
educational, or promotional use. Special editions or
book excerpts can also be created to specification.
For details, please contact your local bookseller
or the Hachette Book Group Special Markets
Department at special.markets@hbgusa.com.

Storey Publishing
210 MASS MoCA Way
North Adams, MA 01247
storey.com

Storey Publishing, LLC is an imprint of Workman
Publishing Co., Inc., a subsidiary of Hachette Book
Group, Inc., 1290 Avenue of the Americas, New
York, NY 10104

ISBNs: 978-1-63586-613-1 (paperback);
978-1-63586-614-8 (ebook)

Printed in China by R. R. Donnelley on paper from
responsible sources
10 9 8 7 6 5 4 3

Library of Congress Cataloging-in-Publication
Data on file

For Leda,
who started me down this path,
lo these many years. I miss you so.

Thanks also to the wonderful team at Storey:
Carleen, Mars, Erin, and Sarah. And as always,
deepest gratitude to Michael, Elizabeth, and
John, my critical readers who have helped
make this book better for everyone.

CONTENTS

The delicate flowers of pineapple weed have loads of flavor!

Forage with Confidence!

Why would anyone want to forage when it's so much easier to go to the grocery store or a favorite neighborhood restaurant? So. Many. Reasons.

Foraging is an amazing way to connect with your local environment, to get to know what grows where in every season. And foraging provides excellent exercise, whether you're climbing mountains or walking through a city park. Personally, I'm in it for the unbuyable flavors. You're never going to find magnolia petals or curly dock seeds at Trader Joe's . . . the only way to experience these flavors is to forage for them yourself! Oh, and one last thing: free food. Who doesn't like free food, especially when it's unique and delicious?

I realize it can be scary starting out. You want to be sure that what you're harvesting is safe before you feed it to your friends and family. (At least I hope you do.) If you feel safe and confident about foraging, you'll do it more often. You may even start to call yourself a forager. And trust me when I tell you that foragers are wonderful people. They care about the environment because they understand their relationship with nature on an intimate level. They love to offer their friends interesting food. And they're generous. They share recipes, favorite foraging spots (usually!), and food processing techniques. That's the kind of person I want to spend time with, and if you're reading this book, I bet you do, too.

When I was choosing plants for this book, I thought very carefully about which wild edible plants would be most useful to the most people. As it says on the cover, this book is for absolute beginners, so I've focused on plants with no poisonous look-alikes (mostly), that are available all over the United States (in general), and that can be used in multiple ways (pretty much always).

This means that I've had to leave out some personal favorites, like cow parsnip (because a beginner might confuse it with giant hogweed), carob (because it grows only in the warmest parts of the country), and hackberry (because the fruit is delish but has limited applications). What I offer in this book is a mere sampling of the many wonderful, delicious, and wild edible plants out there. We all have to start somewhere, right?

In addition to 40 plant profiles, I've included some basics on how plants grow and work because, believe it or not, knowing this will help you be a better forager. I also hope you'll read through the section on safety, because you don't want to make the headlines by poisoning your entire family. You'll also find a brief section on sustainability, because if you're interested in foraging, you understand how important it is to preserve the natural world that makes foraging possible. As a forager, there are things you can do to help protect Mother Earth and her bounty. There is some general info on useful tools for when you're in the field, and at the back of the book are suggestions for preserving your harvest and descriptions of essential kitchen tools, plus a handy list of resources for further reading.

Safety

Many years ago, when my oldest nephew (who now has a master's degree) was very small, he watched me pick serviceberries and asked, "But how do you know they're safe?" I think that's what all of us wonder as we start foraging, and fortunately there are some very simple rules to keep you safe.

First and foremost: Never put anything in your mouth if you're not 100 percent sure what it is. There are no exceptions to this rule. If you're 99 percent sure you know what a plant is, *don't eat it.* Sure, you might miss out on something delicious, but that's a

Sometimes identification characteristics are inside the plant. Moonseeds (shown here) look a lot like grapes, but their seeds are flat and singular, as opposed to grape seeds, which are rounded and multiple.

lot better than sending your entire family to the emergency room because you confused moonseed fruit for grapes.

I suggest a multipronged approach to learning your plants. First, read everything you can get your hands on. (You're already reading this, so good on ya!) Second, join online groups, both regional and national. You'll learn a lot from reading other people's posts, and you can often get help with identification by posting images of your own. And third (I've saved the best for last), get out there and take plant walks with professionals, attend a wild foods gathering, or take a class at a local botanic garden. Nothing builds confidence like hands-on experience, and working with an expert, in person, is the best way to get that.

It takes time to hone your pattern recognition skills, and even experienced foragers sometimes need to check a field guide to be sure of what they've found. How many petals does that flower have? Are the stems hairy? Does the root have a scent? Be slow and methodical, and don't take chances. And be patient. If you can add five or six new plants to your repertoire every year, you'll be feasting on wild edibles in no time.

Okay, so let's say you're now a plant ID maven and can recognize every plant you see. In addition to knowing whether or not a plant is toxic, you need to consider a few other variables.

Location. Where are you foraging? If it's in your own backyard, where you know exactly which chemicals (if any) have been used, you're probably safe. In unknown territory, you'll have to practice your observation skills. Have toxic herbicides been used nearby? Look for swaths of dead or wilted plants, which may indicate a chemical has been used as a weed killer. Some parks post signs when herbicides and insecticides have been applied, but you can't count on this. If the surrounding landscape looks perfect (a golf course? a perfectly groomed rose garden?) the caretakers have probably used chemicals to achieve that look, and those chemicals are probably not things you want to eat.

Permission. I'm not saying I've never popped a black raspberry into my mouth while strolling through Central Park, but in general it's a good idea to have permission from the landowner before you forage, whether it's your next-door neighbor's yucca flowers or the wild plums growing in the nearby national forest. Many state and national lands allow you to harvest small amounts of fruits, nuts, and mushrooms; do an online search for the park's name + "Superintendent's Compendium" to check the rules. In the Valles Caldera, one of my favorite national parks, the rules allow an individual to harvest one pint of things like acorns, pine nuts, and chokecherries, but they must be consumed in the park! I find that oddly fascinating.

Allergies. Do you have food allergies? If you know you're allergic to something, do a little research on what you're foraging. For example, sumac is in the plant family Anacardiaceae, which also includes cashews and mangoes. If you're allergic to cashews or mangoes, you might want to steer clear of sumac fruit. Or start out by tasting a small amount, just to be on the safe side.

A busy road isn't a great foraging location.

Pollution. It's often tempting to harvest from the side of the road, but heavy metals can leach out of vehicle exhaust and be absorbed by plant roots. Roots hold the most pollutants, then stems and leaves, then flowers, fruits, and nuts. These chemicals (such as lead, cadmium, and nickel) tend to travel downslope, washed by rain and snow. So if your Japanese knotweed patch is 50 feet uphill from a busy interstate, it's probably fine. But 50 feet downhill from the same interstate would be borderline in my book. On the other hand, if you're traveling along a quiet country road and spot a field full of milkweed (and if you have permission), go for it!

Seasonality. Some plants should only be harvested at specific times during their growth cycle, not only because they taste better then, but also for safety reasons. Pokeweed must be picked when

A Note on the Seasons

Way back in 1582, the Gregorian calendar set the dates for our seasons according to the movement of the sun. The first day of each season shifts slightly from year to year to accommodate leap years, but basically the first day of each season is the same no matter where you are in the Northern Hemisphere.

This kind of calendar is great for remembering birthdays and doctor's appointments, but isn't the slightest bit helpful to foragers learning what to harvest when. For that, you need to understand on an intuitive, physical level what the seasons are like where *you* forage.

Biological indicators like bud break, fall leaf color, and when the first robin appears or the last monarch departs are much more helpful to a forager learning the seasons. Learn when your average first and last frost dates are, and get to know when the rains come and which microclimates warm up first. When you're familiar with your immediate environment, you'll know when the seasons begin and end by how it feels and what you see, not by a date on the calendar.

it's young and tender or you risk an upset stomach. Underripe persimmons will make the inside of your mouth feel rough and sandpapery. Old banana yucca fruit may have more maggots than flavor.

Preparation. Lots of wild edibles can be enjoyed raw, but not all. The aforementioned pokeweed should only be eaten cooked. Please don't let this put you off pokeweed, because the same is true for some of our favorite grocery store vegetables. Potatoes, some beans, and eggplant can all cause gastric upset when eaten raw.

Also, just as you wash your produce when you bring it home from the grocery store, so should you clean your harvest when you get it back to the kitchen. If you're tasting something on the trail, give it a rinse from your water bottle. And if you're harvesting flowers, be sure to give them a shake to dislodge any insect hitchhikers.

When you take the aforementioned factors into account, foraging is a safe and delicious hobby. A few stats should convince you. The American Association of Poison Control Centers (AAPCC) publishes a report every 2 years listing how many calls they get regarding all sorts of poisonings, including plants and mushrooms. Here are a few quick facts: In the December 2020 report, six deaths were listed in the United States (for 2018 and 2019) related to consumption of poisonous plants. Admittedly, these numbers are only for the US and only include cases where someone actually called a poison control center. But plants are not in the top 20 substance categories responsible for fatal poisonings, and among plants, many of the cases involve things like foxglove, poison ivy, and cherry pits. If you're eating any of these, you are not following my number one rule: Never put anything in your mouth if you're not 100 percent sure what it is.

Got it? Good.

Sustainable Foraging

If I had a dandelion for every time someone said, "But if *everyone* forages for food, we'll wipe out the environment!" . . . well, I'd have a whole lot of dandelions.

The fact is that most foragers are excellent stewards of the natural world. We know we depend on nature if we want to feed ourselves from the wild, and as a result, we are careful with how, when, and what we harvest. To do anything else would be self-sabotage.

The good news is that it's pretty easy to forage sustainably because many delicious wild edibles are considered invasive and can be harvested in large quantities. The USDA defines an invasive

The aerial bulbils of wild garlic often germinate while still on the plant, and look like a crazy hairdo.

plant as "both non-native and able to establish on many sites, grow quickly, and spread to the point of disrupting plant communities or ecosystems." You may hear people refer to some native plants as invasive, but this is inaccurate. Let's call them aggressive rather than invasive.

Aggressive edible plants can usually be harvested in large quantities without risking damage to the plant population. No one will ever complain that you harvested too many sumac berries or too much bee balm. Nor should you worry about overharvesting black locust flowers. Then there's the subject of ramps, a controversial cousin of invasive wild garlic (see Ramp-ing Up on facing page).

If you're not sure something you'd like to harvest is endangered in your area, you can search online (see Resources on page 245 for a list of useful websites). Remember that plant status may vary from one state to the next, meaning that you should look for local information.

Ramp-ing Up

Even if you've never foraged, you've probably heard people talk about ramps. Some claim that ramp bulbs should never be harvested and that foragers should take only a single leaf from a plant. Others believe that healthy ramp populations benefit from regular harvesting of the entire plant.

So which is it? While it's true that some commercial harvesters (I don't call them foragers) pillage their local ramp populations without considering the consequences, in other locations, ramp populations are actually increasing. Sam Thayer, the most accomplished and best-known forager in the United States today, has conducted the longest-running ramp population study in the US, which shows that, overall, ramp populations have increased in the last 100 years. In areas where ramp populations have decreased, it is not due to foraging, but rather the expansion of agricultural land use and the increase in garlic mustard populations. Sam concludes that ramps can be sustainably harvested in areas with ideal growing conditions. Thinning a large ramp patch improves the chances of seed germination, which leads to population growth.

All of this means that you'll have to evaluate your local ramp population for yourself. If you're surrounded by acres of ramps, feel free to harvest responsibly. If you've found a single plant in the nearby woods, let it live to propagate itself and check back in a few years. In the meantime, forage for wild garlic to your heart's content. It's super abundant, very similar in flavor to ramps, and considered invasive throughout the US.

Allium tricoccum

Three Ways to Forage Mindfully

In addition to being savvy about plants with endangered or protected status, you can do a few other things to assist Mother Nature in maintaining the populations of edible plants.

1. **Pull the bullies.** If you notice an aggressive or invasive edible (like garlic mustard) encroaching on a clump of something with a less aggressive growth habit (like wild ginger), pull up some of that garlic mustard, even if it's not the perfect time to take it back to your kitchen.

2. **When you gather roots, spread seeds.** If you're harvesting a plant for its root, bulb, or tuber and there are seeds present on the plant, scratch a clear space in the surrounding soil and scatter those seeds to help propagate the plant. Since fall is one of the best times to harvest roots, and since that's also when seeds have ripened on most plants, this is easy to do.

3. **Remember: It's not all about you.** You're not the only forager out there; leave enough behind for animals, and for the species to propagate itself. There's no specific recommended percentage here, because how much you can sustainably harvest will depend on the population of the plant in question and how many animals (including humans) depend on the plant for food. It's hard not to be greedy when you come across a clump of something delicious, but remember that you're not the only one who's hungry.

The most important takeaway here is that we are connected to nature, not opposed to it. As such, we need to help conserve the beauty, the wonder, and, yes, the food, that our environment provides. Because we foragers generally have a close personal relationship with our local environment, we care deeply about making sure our natural surroundings are healthy and respected. When you love something, you don't destroy it. You do everything you can to help it thrive.

Plant Parts

I promise this is not a botany lesson! But once you understand a little about plant anatomy, you'll find it easier to identify and eat wild edible plants. Let's start from the ground up.

ROOTS

Root crops are generally either thick taproots, tubers, or bulbs. Sound confusing? Carrots are taproots, potatoes are tubers, and onions are bulbs. They are best harvested in either early spring or late fall, when the plants are not in active growth. Plants draw on the stored nutrition in their roots (or tubers or bulbs) during the growing season, so they'll be at their biggest and best either at the end of the season (when nutrition has been stored for next year's growth), or at the beginning of the season (before the plant has begun to put out shoots and leaves).

Before you harvest any root crops, you must first be sure that the soil is not polluted, as root crops absorb and store both water and nutrients from the surrounding soil. Don't harvest root crops close to a busy road, or anywhere herbicides have been sprayed. This is true for foraging in general, but especially so for root crops.

evening primrose roots

STEMS

Stem crops are best harvested when they are young, tender, and flexible. Older stems become fibrous and tough. Think about how we discard the bottoms of asparagus stems, choosing to eat the more tender top growth. Have you ever ordered bamboo in a Chinese restaurant? No, you have not. You have ordered bamboo *shoots*—the young, tender new growth of the bamboo. Mature bamboo is woody and distinctly unappetizing . . . unless you're a panda.

But wait! There's an exception to that rule! If the tip of a stem crop is still soft and flexible, it's edible, even if the plant is no longer young. When the cells in the tips of plant stems are dividing and growing rapidly, we call this meristematic growth (okay, I know that sounds a lot like a botany lesson, but stay with me here). Meristematic growth is tender and flexible and exactly what you're looking for in an edible stem. When you bend a stalk of asparagus to find the place where tender meets tough, you're looking for the meristematic part of the plant because *that* is what you want to eat. Meristematic growth usually happens in spring, but it can continue a little longer in some wild plants.

This Japanese knotweed is at the perfect stage for harvesting.

lamb's quarters

LEAVES

Leaf crops are easy to understand. We've all made a salad or sautéed some leafy greens, and it's pretty intuitive to make the shift from store-bought spinach to wild lamb's quarters (a.k.a. wild spinach). When it comes to identifying leaf crops in the field, you'll need to look at several different things.

- Are the leaves arranged opposite each other on the stem or do they alternate?

- What do the edges of the leaves (a.k.a. leaf margins) look like? They may be smooth, scalloped, or toothed.

- Does the leaf have its own stem? This is called a petiole, and in many cases it can be eaten, too. Rhubarb and celery are both actually leaf petioles.

Get to Know Leaves

When describing leaves and leaf shapes, I've used a few botanical terms (sorry, not sorry) you'll need to understand.

BRACT: a modified leaf surrounding a flower, often mistaken for the flower itself; the poinsettia is a common example of a plant with bracts (red, modified leaves) surrounding small flowers (tiny yellow flowers you may never have noticed)

COMPOUND: a leaf with several sections growing from a central stem

ELLIPTICAL: a leaf shaped like an ellipse, that is, widest in the middle and somewhat equal on both ends

LANCEOLATE: a leaf shaped like a lance head, with the widest part near the base

LEAFLET: a segment of a compound leaf

OCREA: a sheath at the base of a leaf stem

PALMATE: a leaf that has lobes or divisions originating from a single point, like the palm of your hand

PINNATE: small leaflets arranged along a central stem

SPATULATE: a leaf with a tip that is broader than its base (like a spatula!)

whitetop mustard flowers

sumac berries

FLOWERS

Flower crops are more prevalent than you might expect. Everyone recognizes a flower petal used as a garnish, but most commercial garnishes are chosen for their looks rather than their flavor. Some wild blooms (I'm looking at you, plum blossom!) have wonderful flavors that infuse well in cream, syrup, and vinegar.

Have you ever eaten a stuffed zucchini blossom? Well, you can do the same thing with yucca flowers. And if you've ever eaten broccoli, then you've eaten immature flower buds. I highly recommend looking for broccoli's better-tasting cousin, whitetop mustard. You'll notice the family resemblance immediately.

FRUITS

Most of the wild edible fruits detailed in this book are closely related to their cultivated cousins, so they will be easy for you to recognize. Mallow fruits, milkweed pods, sumac berries, Siberian elm samaras, and rose hips are less recognizable, but they are all totally worth getting to know.

While you should take special care to avoid harvesting root crops from polluted soils, you don't need to take the same care with fruits and flowers. Because fruits and flowers are the plant parts farthest away from the soil, and because water and nutrition have to travel up through the roots, stems, and leaves before getting to them, these last two plant parts may occasionally be harvested from a moderately used roadside. Don't make a habit of it, but if you've found the perfect persimmon tree on a neighborhood street, you have my permission to harvest. If it's within 10 feet of a busy highway . . . not so much.

A Note on Ripeness

Some fruits look ripe long before they actually are, so it's important to use your senses of touch, smell, and taste, as well as your eyes when determining if a wild fruit is ready to harvest. For example, a ripe mulberry will fall into your hand at the slightest touch. It may look ripe a week earlier, but don't rely on the color alone. If you have to pull a deep purple berry off the tree, you'll be disappointed in the flavor, despite the fact that it *looks* ready. Sumac is another fruit that looks ripe, with bright red berries, long before its sour flavor has fully developed. So be prepared to give fruit a sniff, a taste, and a squeeze. If it's fragrant or sweet or soft, that's important information that will help you forage more deliciously.

Foraging Tools

The right tool can make short work of a long task. Here's a list of what I consider to be essential foraging tools. Start with these, and add your own favorites as you go along.

BYPASS PRUNERS

If you're a forager who wants to harvest from the same crop periodically, or if you simply care about the health of the plants you're harvesting from, get yourself a good set of bypass pruners. Bypass pruners have one sharp blade that slides by another to make a clean cut, allowing for undamaged future growth. Avoid anvil pruners, which crush the stem and impede future growth.

HORI-HORI KNIFE

Sometimes called a soil knife, the hori-hori is a Japanese tool with a serrated blade on one side and a smooth blade on the other. It's perfect for digging around a root crop like dandelion roots. The serrated edge cuts through soil and roots easily, and it can also be used to pry up a root system. Get one with a scabbard to protect yourself from unintentional slicing of human flesh.

SCISSORS

Some things, like tender stems and leaves, are better cut with scissors than with pruners.

TROWEL

A garden trowel is handy for digging up shallow roots and tubers.

BAGS

I forage with a stash of plastic grocery bags in my backpack so I can keep my harvested crops separate and clean. Why put dirty field garlic bulbs in with garlic mustard? If you live somewhere that doesn't allow stores to distribute plastic bags, use paper or cloth bags.

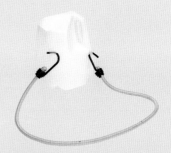

BLICKY

I hesitate to use this word because the internet tells me it means something else entirely (go look it up). For foragers, however, a blicky is a container (such as a gallon milk jug with the top cut off) we strap to our waist that leaves both hands free for harvesting. It's especially useful for berries.

SOLID BACKPACK OR BASKET

Unless you want to telegraph where all your best spots are, keep that harvest to yourself with a pack you can't see through!

WATER BOTTLE

Yes, you need to stay hydrated. But a little splash of water also lets you rinse dirt off your harvest in the field. A water bottle is also especially handy if you'd like to clean something before tasting it as a trail nibble.

BUG DOPE

Depending on where you forage, you'll have different insects and ticks to deal with. Choose the right bug repellent for your area. I soak my foraging outfit in permethrin to repel ticks. Works like a charm.

GLOVES

Imagine that you stumble across a huge patch of perfectly tender nettles, but you don't have your gloves. You'd probably figure something out, but why not be prepared?

CHAPTER 1

WILD EDIBLES
That Grow Just about Everywhere

No kidding. I've found these plants from Alaska to Florida and just about everywhere in between. Sun or shade, lawn or gravel, these are tough, persistent plants that take hold wherever they can.

DANDELION

Taraxacum officinale, T. erythrospermum

A.k.a.: blowball, faceclock, lion's tooth

Best part to eat: leaves, roots, flower petals

When to harvest: spring (leaves, roots), summer (flowers), fall (leaves, roots)

Dandelions elicit strong negative reactions from lawn lovers and gardeners. But foragers love this plant because it provides four (count 'em, four!) delicious edible parts. There are many species of dandelion, and some are native to the United States. However, the most common species (*Taraxacum officinale* and *T. erythrospermum)* are native to Europe. All dandelions can be used in the same way.

Colonists brought dandelions from Europe to America as a food and medicinal plant, yet centuries later we see it as merely a weed. Today, most conversations about dandelions revolve around eliminating them . . . as if that were possible!

The name *dandelion* comes from the French words *dent de lion*, meaning tooth of the lion. The teeth on the leaves are an essential identification

Fresh dandelion greens are best harvested in cool weather.

factor for the dandelion: They point backward toward the center of the plant. Other weeds with toothed leaves arranged in a basal rosette (dandelion look-alikes such as cat's ear, false dandelion, and wild lettuce) have leaves with notches that point forward, away from the center of the plant. The depth of the teeth on dandelion leaves varies greatly from plant to plant, but those teeth always point back toward the center of the plant.

Dandelions produce one yellow flower per stem, and their stems are straight, never branching. A single plant may put up more than one stem per plant, but dandelion stems never branch or bear more than one flower at a time. The dandelion look-alikes mentioned earlier have branching stems and often produce multiple flowers simultaneously.

Dandelions are cool-weather greens; they will be less bitter in winter, spring, and fall. Roots should be harvested in late fall or early spring, when the plant is not in active growth.

FEASTING

Leaves. Dandelion leaves are a classic bitter green, packed with minerals and vitamins. Young dandelion leaves are slightly bitter, like chicory or endive. They can be eaten raw in salads, balanced with mild greens. Summer dandelion greens are usually too bitter to be enjoyed raw, but cooking extends the dandelion season. Blanch dandelion leaves for 2 to 3 minutes to remove some of the bitterness, then combine them with milder greens in egg dishes, stir-fries, or pitas.

Flowers. Harvest tightly closed dandelion flower buds when they're still at ground level, tucked into the center of the leaves. The bracts that surround the flower bud can be bitter, so peel them off the bottom of the buds. Dandelion flower buds can be pickled or blanched for a minute or two, then served with butter, salt, and pepper.

Dandelion petals can be baked into cookies and quick breads, used to make jelly (page 238), or added to spring rolls for a burst of color. They don't have much flavor, but they sure look nice. My favorite way to use dandelion petals is in wine (page 236). Harvest fully opened flowers, then remove the bracts by holding the base of the petals in one hand, the bracts in the other, and twisting your hands in opposite directions, separating the petals from the bracts.

Roots. Harvest dandelion taproots in late fall or early spring, when they're plump and full of nutrition. Young roots can be boiled and eaten as a vegetable (older roots may be woody and tough), but their taste is mild and, to me, not particularly interesting. Instead, try roasting your dandelion roots to make a flavorful, caffeine-free beverage. Or, if you've got a sweet tooth, infuse the roasted roots in cream (page 240) and use it to make one of the most delicious ice cream flavors you might ever taste! (It's one of my favorites, and I have tasted a lot of ice cream.) Dandelion roots also make great homemade bitters.

DANDELION
KNOW BEFORE YOU EAT

WHERE AND HOW TO FIND

- Grows in every state of the US and across the temperate zones
- Will grow in sun or shade but flowers best in full sun
- Perennial plants with thick taproots that hold water and nutrition, allowing them to grow in dry, poor soils as well as almost everywhere else

ID CHECKLIST

- Plants produce a basal rosette of foliage in early spring.
- Leaves are smooth, strongly toothed, and teeth point back toward the center of the plant.
- Plants may be small (3–4 inches in diameter) with foliage that hugs the ground, or large (10–12 inches in diameter) with upright foliage.
- Individual leaves can be 2–10 inches long.
- Plants produce one flower per stem and stems do not branch.
- Flowers are yellow, becoming more orange toward the center.
- Flowers are 1–2 inches in diameter, and close up at night.
- Flower stems are smooth, leafless, and hollow, and ooze a white sap when broken, as do the leaves.
- Flower petals are surrounded at the base by green bracts.
- Flowers are succeeded by round seed heads.

The teeth on dandelion leaves point back toward the center of the plant.

Dandelion stems and foliage ooze a white sap when cut.

DOCK

Rumex crispus, R. obtusifolius

A.k.a.: curly dock, bitter dock, broad-leaved dock

Best part to eat: leaves, seeds

When to harvest: spring (leaves), fall (new leaves and seeds)

Docks were widely eaten during the Great Depression, and appreciated for their tart, lemony flavor; their abundance; and the fact that they were free for the taking. Today most people have forgotten about this common and tasty edible plant. It's so sad.

Docks are perennials, most often found in sunny ground. Their taproot makes them quite drought tolerant, but their foliage growth is more lush and tender with more moisture. Dock grows as a basal rosette of foliage in early spring and is one of the first greens to emerge. One of the best identification features is a small, thin sheath that covers the base of each leaf. This is the ocrea, and it turns brown as the plant ages.

By early summer, dock produces tall flower stalks that bear copious amounts of seeds. These stalks often remain standing over winter and serve as an excellent marker when you're foraging for young dock greens in spring.

FEASTING

The sour flavor of dock comes from oxalic acid, which may cause kidney stones when consumed in large quantities. The same compound is found in spinach. If your doctor has advised you not to eat spinach or if you are prone to kidney stones, don't eat dock. If you are generally healthy and don't gorge yourself on multiple pounds of dock every day for a month, you should be fine. If you are nervous about this, err on the side of caution.

Because dock has a short harvest season, harvest it at its peak, then blanch for 60 seconds and freeze for later use. Dock is considered an invasive weed in 15 states, so you probably won't make a dent in the local population.

Leaves. The small leaves at the center of the plant are the tastiest, and the unfurled, youngest leaves are the prize! Young leaves are tasty raw or cooked. If you want to use them raw, the mucilage may be a little overwhelming, so remove the leaf stem and use only the leaves themselves in salads. Larger leaf stems may be chopped and

Go for the youngest leaves at the center of the dock plant.

cooked as a substitute for rhubarb or Japanese knotweed.

Like so many greens, dock reduces in volume when cooked, to about 20 to 25 percent of its original volume. The application of heat also changes dock's texture from slightly papery to creamy, and the color from bright green to a dull brownish-green. Cooking may transform the slight bitterness in raw leaves into mild lemony deliciousness, so if your raw harvest tastes only slightly bitter, consider using it as a cooked green.

Dock greens are excellent boiled or sautéed in stir-fries, soups, stews, and egg dishes. I especially love dock with cream and cheese, not just because cream and cheese are delicious, but because something about the texture and flavor of cooked dock works wonderfully with dairy.

Seeds. Dock seeds can be dried, roasted, and ground to make a gluten-free flour—no winnowing necessary! (Separating the seeds from their husks—i.e. winnowing—can be very tedious!) Some people consider the seeds to be too bitter, but I disagree.

Roots. The root of curly dock is yellow and intensely bitter. While it has traditionally been used for medicinal purposes, I prefer to use it in cocktail bitters. You can use the root fresh or dried.

OTHER SPECIES

There are many edible docks, but they are less widespread than curly dock and broad-leaved dock. Others include western dock (*Rumex occidentalis*), yard dock (*R. longifolius*), and field dock (*R. stenophyllus*). Wild rhubarb (*R. hymenosepalus*) is common in the desert Southwest and is larger and more succulent than many other docks. Patience dock (*R. patientia*) was once cultivated as a vegetable in both the United States and Europe and is still grown by savvy gardeners. If you read about a green called patience, you're reading about patience dock.

These dock seeds are enclosed in a papery sheath.

Bitter dock and broad dock are two common names for the same plant: *R. obtusifolius*.

WHERE AND HOW TO FIND

- Grows best in full sun to part shade
- Thrives with moisture (though will tolerate drought), so check moist spots first
- Harvest tender young foliage in early spring and again in fall.
- Harvest ripe dock seeds in late summer to early fall.
- Look for last year's tall seed stalks to spot fresh, new growth.

ID CHECKLIST

- Grows a basal rosette of foliage in early spring; mature plants may grow to be 1–3 feet tall.
- Leaves include a clasping, mucilaginous ocrea at the base.
- Individual leaves may be 12–18 inches long.
- Leaves on flowering stem are generally much smaller than basal rosette foliage.
- Look for lots and lots of mucilage (hands will be covered with slimy, sticky mucilage when harvesting).
- Mature leaves of curly dock are usually narrow with wavy leaf margins.
- Young curly dock foliage has less wavy margins and may be less narrow than mature foliage.
- Mature leaves of broad-leaved dock may have a slightly wavy leaf margin, and are broader than those of curly dock.

Note the flower spike starting to form at the center of the plant. This plant may be too tough to be delicious.

- Leaves may show red discoloration when bruised or punctured by insects or animals (if otherwise young and fresh, they are fine to eat).
- Seeds ripen from pale green to deep, reddish-brown.
- Each seed is enclosed in a thin membrane.
- Flower/seed stalks may mature to be over 5 feet tall.

MUGWORT

Artemisia vulgaris

A.k.a.: chrysanthemum weed, common wormwood, moxa

Best part to eat: leaves

When to harvest: before flowering

Mugwort foliage looks a lot like chrysanthemum foliage, which is also edible. Mugwort leaves are 2 to 4 inches long, medium green on top, whitish underneath, and deeply lobed. Rub the leaves between your fingers and you'll notice a strong herbal smell. If the leaf you're rubbing doesn't have a strong smell, it's not mugwort!

Unlike chrysanthemums, there will be no showy flowers come fall. In mid- to late summer, mugwort produces long, feathery, terminal clusters of small, reddish-green flowers. Mature plants may be over 3 feet tall (before flowering), but the leaves and stems will be fibrous at this point, although the roots are still useful. Mugwort is a perennial herb, dying back to the ground every year and regrowing from the roots.

Mugwort leaves are most tender and tasty in spring, before the plant flowers. This is less important if you plan to dry and grind the herb, but if you're going to use it fresh, young leaves are the way to go. Mugwort foliage is highly variable. Leaves near the top of the plant are more deeply divided, with thinner lobes than the basal leaves.

The roots of mugwort are long and woody and may spread quite some distance underground, sending up new shoots along the way. They make an excellent base for cocktail bitters.

FEASTING

I don't understand why more foragers don't write about mugwort. It's truly delicious, and since it's so easy to harvest in massive quantities, there's no excuse not to use it. The flavor reminds me of sage, but it's more interesting than that. It combines well with ginger, garlic, and sesame.

Mugwort has a long history in herbal medicine, and many cultures also use it as a cooking herb. In Europe it's used with fatty meats such as goose, duck,

Compare these young leaves, which are less deeply divided, to the more mature leaves (more finely and deeply divided) on page 38.

and pork. It's also a traditional flavoring in multiple Asian cuisines. We pay good money for mugwort noodles and mugwort mochi in specialty grocery stores, yet most people ignore the fact that this rampant weed grows all around us.

Leaves. Mugwort can be used fresh or dried. Fresh leaves can be chopped and used in salads and stir-fries, or as the basis for a flavorful soup.

If you're going to use it dry, be aware that dried mugwort needs some special treatment. You may dry mugwort like any other herb (keep temperatures below 95°F [35°C] to preserve as many essential oils as possible), but

unlike most dried herbs, ground mugwort doesn't form a powder. Instead it becomes fluffy, like cotton wool. (Really, it looks more like green dryer lint, but that doesn't sound very appetizing.)

If you want to cook with ground mugwort, you'll need to rehydrate it. Transfer the ground mugwort to a bowl and add enough water to hydrate the herb. You'll have to stir it around a bit because the ground mugwort is so light that it floats on top of the water. Once it's been hydrated, pour the herb into a strainer and press on it to remove as much water as possible.

CAUTION: AVOID IF PREGNANT

Historically, one of mugwort's medicinal uses has been to regulate menstruation. It may cause uterine contractions and should therefore be avoided by anyone hoping to become or remain pregnant.

Some people confuse mugwort with ragweed (*Ambrosia artemisiifolia*), and the Latin name of that plant tells you why. *Artemisiifolia* means "with leaves that look like artemisia," and a side-by-side comparison shows this is true. Nonetheless, it's easy to tell the two plants apart once you know what to look for: Ragweed's leaves are much more finely divided. Paleoarcheologists have discovered that ragweed species were harvested (and maybe even cultivated) by Indigenous peoples. Ragweed seeds were used as a grain and are high in protein and oil. Modern foragers don't generally consider ragweed to be a choice edible. The foliage is bitter and the seeds require extensive processing. Don't worry, if you misidentify ragweed as mugwort, you won't poison yourself, and the first bitter bite will let you know you've made a mistake!

The leaves of ragweed are similar to, but definitely not identical to, the leaves of mugwort.

KNOW BEFORE YOU EAT

WHERE AND HOW TO FIND

- Thrives where many other plants do not: in highly compacted, disturbed soils
- A perennial plant that spreads by underground rhizomes as well as by seed
- Often forms thick clumps
- Tolerates a wide range of growing conditions but thrives in full sun

ID CHECKLIST

- Plants may grow to be 3–5 feet tall.

- Foliage is highly variable, but all leaves are dark green on top and whitish underneath; overall effect is gray-green.

- Tops of leaves are smooth (hairless); undersides are covered with short hairs.

- Leaves are 2–4 inches long, arranged alternately on the stem.

- Crushed leaves emit a strong, spicy smell.

- All foliage is lobed, but early foliage is less deeply divided than foliage higher up on stem.

- Stems are covered with fuzzy white hairs when young.

- Stems become less hairy and develop a purple color with age.

- Small, greenish-red flowers appear in late summer to early autumn.

- Flowers are held in feathery terminal clusters.

flower clusters

The undersides of leaves are white.

OXEYE DAISY

Leucanthemum vulgare, formerly Chrysanthemum leucanthemum

A.k.a.: marguerite, dog daisy, field daisy

Best part to eat: leaves

When to harvest: any time

Is it a weed? Is it a pretty garden flower? In my book, oxeye daisy is an attractive perennial with tasty leaves, edible flowers, and (I'll admit it) an aggressive growth habit. Native to Europe, it has naturalized across North America and some people consider it a pest in the garden. I am not one of those people. Oxeye daisy has a relatively shallow root system and isn't difficult to pull up, although new plants will grow from any piece of rhizome left behind. If you have it (and don't want it) in your garden, pull it up and bring the leaves into the kitchen.

You may read that oxeye daisy prefers a consistently moist soil, and you certainly will find it growing where rainfall is generous. However, you will also find it growing in every state of the union (including Alaska and Hawaii!). I see it frequently when I'm hiking in New Mexico, which is not a rainy state. In other words, this is an adaptable plant!

Oxeye daisy grows first as a basal rosette of glossy, deep green foliage, with scalloped leaf margins. In early summer the plant produces one or more flowering stems. The composite flower of the oxeye daisy is made up of white, sterile petals (called ray flowers) and a yellow, fertile center (composed of multiple disc flowers).

Basal leaves are larger and juicier than the stem leaves, and the basal rosette overwinters in milder climates. Oxeye daisy foliage can be harvested any time it looks fresh. Unlike many other greens, its flavor does not decline after the flowers bloom.

Since oxeye daisies are often found in abundance, you should be able to pick plenty of foliage while leaving the plants intact; just spread your harvest among several plants. Several states (Montana, Colorado, Ohio, Washington, Wyoming) have classified the oxeye daisy as a noxious weed, and some have forbidden commercial sales of the plant. It is highly unlikely you'll make a dent in the oxeye daisy population.

FEASTING

Leaves. The leaves are the tastiest part of this plant. Nibble one before harvesting a batch, to be sure you like the flavor. It's slightly succulent, and it's a little stronger than mild greens like lamb's quarters and stinging nettles, but not bitter like dandelions or wintercress. The flavor is an interesting combination of spinach, lemon, and pepper, and it enlivens mild greens and balances bitter ones. You'll probably never make an entire dish out of the leaves (although you could if you love them and find an abundant patch), but they are invaluable to the forager who appreciates unique flavors.

Cooked oxeye daisy foliage mixes well with other greens in pies, soups, stews, and quesadillas, but raw oxeye daisy foliage is where the flavor really shines. It's snappy tucked into sandwiches and mixed with other greens in salads.

Flowers. The yellow disc flowers in the center of the flower are edible, but I don't like the texture so I don't eat them. Pluck the white petals as soon as the blooms have fully opened. They don't have a ton of flavor, but they make an attractive addition to a salad.

OXEYE DAISY
KNOW BEFORE YOU EAT

Oxeye daisy petals make a decorative salad ingredient.

WHERE AND HOW TO FIND

- Full-sun, perennial plant
- Will tolerate some shade in hot climates
- Flowers less abundantly in shade, but since the foliage is the tastiest part, this isn't a problem
- Spread by rhizomes and by seed, and may form thick clumps

ID CHECKLIST

- Plants form a basal rosette of foliage in spring.
- Leaves are dark green and shiny, and tips are broader than leaf base, like a spatula (spatulate).
- Foliage is 3–5 inches long.
- Leaf margins are scalloped.

Scalloped leaf margins are clearly visible on this basal rosette.

- Flower spike has smaller leaves arranged alternately on the stem.
- Plants are 2–3 feet tall when in flower.
- Plants bloom from mid-spring through summer, depending on where you forage.
- Flowers have white petals surrounding yellow center.
- Foliage may overwinter in mild climates; may be harvested year-round.

Oxeye daisies are easy to identify at this stage.

SIBERIAN ELM

Ulmus pumila

A.k.a.: Asiatic elm, dwarf elm, Manchurian elm

Best part to eat: samaras (seeds)

When to harvest: spring, when the samaras are green and flexible

The Siberian elm is among the toughest of trees. Native to Siberia, Mongolia, northern Kashmir, and the Gobi Desert (among other rugged locations), it was selected by the USDA to create shelterbelts on the American prairies after the disaster that was the dust bowl. Its tolerance for cold and drought and its rapid growth habit made it the perfect candidate for erosion control and soil retention. Oops! This tree has since spread across most of the United States (except, in general, the Southeast) and is widely considered invasive. Nonetheless, it is still used for shade and windbreaks.

Siberian elm requires lots of sunlight, so you probably won't find it in a shady wooded spot. This is a tree of open fields and sunny waste spaces, like along railroad tracks, and on the edges of parking lots and playgrounds. Young Siberian elms are often multistemmed trees, and when these are cut back repeatedly they will maintain this juvenile growth habit for years, resprouting from the cut tree trunk.

Siberian elm is a short-lived tree (as trees go), with trees outside of Siberia living about 60 years. But since it grows very quickly, it can reach a mature height of 70 feet in good growing conditions. Its bark is rough, furrowed, and chunky. Leaves are deep green on top, with paler undersides. They are elliptical in shape, about 1 to 2½ inches long, with toothed leaf margins, and arranged alternately on branches. The seeds of the Siberian elm are called samaras. Each mature Siberian elm produces thousands of samaras, which emerge before the leaves do, giving the branches a frilly appearance. The samara consists of a seed surrounded by a papery, round covering about ½ inch in diameter. Samaras emerge pale green and ripen to dry brown.

samaras

young leaves

While Siberian elm is considered invasive in many states, it continues to be sold commercially. I get it. If you live someplace dry, windy, with extreme hot and cold temperatures, where the soil is poor and trees are hard to come by, you appreciate the shade of any tree, whether or not someone tells you it's invasive. I live in New Mexico, the only state in the US to categorize Siberian elm as a noxious weed (as of this writing), and I do my part to limit the spread of this tree by eating as many samaras as possible every spring.

FEASTING

Seeds. The samaras of the Siberia elm are where it's at! The season is short and this isn't a wild food that is easy to preserve, so I suggest you enjoy them fresh while they're in season. The flavor is light, green, almost sweet, and nutty, and the texture is an interesting combination of delicate papery covering and dense, nutty center. Siberian elm samaras are tasty raw and make an interesting trail nibble, but my favorite way to use them is in rice and pasta dishes, or with eggs in a scramble or quiche. Samaras don't require long cooking, so toss them into your pasta or rice or eggs a few minutes before you finish cooking. Harvest fresh samaras when they are pale green and tender. If the papery casing has turned brown, it's no longer delicious.

I've heard foragers talk about drying the samaras, winnowing the seeds from their papery casings, and eating the mature seeds raw, or using dried seeds as a lentil substitute. I have yet to try this. I want to. I really do. But it sounds like a *lot* of work. Maybe next year.

Leaves. While some foragers consider the young leaves of Siberian elm to be edible, I don't think they're worth it. The texture is fine (when foliage has just unfurled and is very tender), but there isn't much flavor to speak of, so why bother, unless you're in need of bulk greens.

LOOK-ALIKE

Some people confuse Siberian elm with Chinese elm (*Ulmus parvifolia*), which also produces edible samaras, but the visual differences are very obvious. The bark of Chinese elm is smooth, mottled, and exfoliating, revealing patches of gray and red. This interesting pattern is quite beautiful and gives the tree the common name of lacebark elm. Siberian elm has gray-brown, roughly furrowed bark and is much more ordinary-looking. Also, Chinese elm is a smaller tree, growing to about 30 to 40 feet tall, and it produces its samaras in fall, not spring.

Chinese elm

WHERE AND HOW TO FIND

- Look in dry, sunny open spots.
- Tree is easiest to spot when it's decked out with light green samaras in spring.
- It's easiest to harvest samaras before leaves unfurl; simply slide your hand down the branch to collect your harvest without also pulling the leaves off the tree.
- Harvest samaras in spring, while still pale green throughout.

Notice how the seeds in the center of these samaras have turned brown? That means they're past their prime.

ID CHECKLIST

- Pale green samaras cover tree branches before leaves emerge.
- Leaves are approximately 1 inch wide and 2½ inches long, with toothed margins.
- Foliage is alternately arranged along branches.
- Leaf base is uneven.
- Mature trees are usually single stemmed.
- Immature trees look like shrubs, with multiple stems.
- Wood is brittle and susceptible to breaking under heavy snow or wind.
- Look for broken branches, especially near the top of the tree.

Siberian elm leaves

immature Siberian elm

Siberian elm bark

SOW THISTLE

Sonchus oleraceus, S. arvensis, S. asper

A.k.a.: field sow thistle, prickly sow thistle, hare thistle, hare lettuce, milky tassel

Best part to eat: leaves

When to harvest: before flowers emerge in spring or early summer

There are three types of sow thistle common to the United States and all three have at least one tasty part. Don't be put off by the prickly-looking stems and leaves. A quick blanch will soften them right up and make them an excellent, mild-flavored green.

The most common species of sow thistle in the US are the annual common sow thistle (*Sonchus oleraceus*) and the perennial field sow thistle (*S. arvensis*). Prickly sow thistle (*S. asper)* is also common, but its leaf margins are too prickly for me and I can't be bothered to trim each leaf. Its stems, however, are worth harvesting.

Sow thistles have a basal rosette of foliage and ooze a white sap when the leaves or stems are broken. Their stems are hollow. Also, sow thistles are cool-weather plants, meaning they are most tender and tasty in cool weather. Sow thistle is usually bitter in hot weather and should be cooked to remove bitterness. The leaves of the different sow thistles have different shapes, although all are lobed, with the terminal lobe being much larger than the side lobes.

Oh, and sow thistles are not true thistles. Sow thistles are in the genus *Sonchus* and true thistles are in *Cirsium, Carduus,* and *Onopordum*. So if you harvest sow thistle foliage and tell your friends they're eating thistle leaves (leaving off the "sow"), that would be wrong.

LOOK-ALIKES

Some people confuse sow thistles with dandelions, but there are several easy ways to tell the two apart. Dandelions have only one flower per stem and the flower stems never branch. Sow thistles produce more than one flower per stem and the flower stems branch near the top. Additionally, the flower stems of dandelions never have leaves, while

sow thistle

dandelion

Left: Sow thistle produces multiple flowers on branching stems. *Right:* Dandelions produce single flowers on non-branching stems.

the flower stems of sow thistle stems have leaves that clasp the stem. If you still confuse the two, don't worry—since both are edible, you won't make a fatal mistake.

Sow thistles may also resemble some wild lettuces (also edible). Both sow thistle and wild lettuce ooze white sap when broken, and some lettuces have yellow flowers similar to those of sow thistle. Check the back of the midrib of a leaf, and if there is a line of prickles running down the midrib, that's wild lettuce, not sow thistle. The prickles of sow thistle are relegated to the leaf margins.

Wild lettuce foliage (shown above) resembles that of sow thistle, but wild lettuce leaves have prickles along the midrib, while sow thistle foliage has prickles along the leaf margins.

FEASTING

Leaves. The leaves of young sow thistle plants can be eaten raw in salads and sandwiches; consider them a pleasantly bitter green. As the foliage matures, you'll probably want to briefly boil or sauté the leaves to reduce both the prick of the prickles and the bitterness. Use it in any way you'd use spinach. The flavor of sow thistle leaves varies greatly depending on the location, temperature, and sunlight, so taste a leaf or two before making a massive harvest.

Stems. The flower stem of sow thistle is the tastiest part of this plant. Stems of common sow thistle are generally too thin to make them worthwhile, but field sow thistle and prickly sow thistle both produce heftier stems. Cut the stem close to the ground before the plant flowers, and take a bite. If it's a little bitter, peel the stem before eating it raw or cooked. Not all sow thistle stems require this step. And don't feel bad about cutting off the flower stalk before the sow thistle has a chance to reproduce; these plants are extremely good at reproducing and you won't make a dent in their population.

Buds. Unopened flower buds can be pickled and used like capers. I'm not against the principle of pickling, but I think most pickles taste like the brine they're pickled in rather than the thing that's being pickled. Anyway, this seems like a waste of foraging time to me. If you're just going to taste brine, go buy yourself a jar of kosher dills.

Roots. Technically, the roots of sow thistle are edible, but I don't know anyone who thinks they're tasty. So if you're lost and starving, go for it. Otherwise, never mind.

buds

root

WHERE AND HOW TO FIND

- Look in open fields, cracks in the pavement, parks, roadsides, and gardens.
- Plants grow best in full sun, but shade-growing sow thistles are tenderest and tastiest.
- Harvest young leaves in cool weather for least bitterness; harvest field sow thistle and prickly sow thistle flower stems in summer.

ID CHECKLIST

- Young foliage forms a basal rosette.
- Foliage is toothed, edged with prickles, and the teeth point back toward the center of the plant.
- Leaves clasp the flower stem directly, rather than attach to the stem with a leaf stem (important identification characteristic).
- Leaves are arranged alternately on flower stem and are less deeply lobed than basal leaves; some are not lobed at all.

basal rosette

See how the leaf attaches directly to the stem.

- Basal leaves are 4–12 inches long; leaves on flower stems are smaller.
- Leaves and stems ooze white sap when broken.
- Leaf color may change from medium green to dark green, and may eventually show shades of purple as plant grows.
- Flower stems may turn purple with maturity.
- Yellow flowers of perennial sow thistle are ½–1 inch in diameter.
- Yellow flowers of annual sow thistle are smaller and not as bright as perennial sow thistle.
- Plants branch at the top of their flower stems.
- Plants produce fluffy seed heads, similar to those of dandelions.
- Mature plants may be 1–4 feet tall in bloom.

Note the multiple flowers on a single stem; this is an important identification characteristic.

WILD GARLIC

Allium vineale

A.k.a.: field garlic, onion grass, crow garlic

Best part to eat: bulbs

When to harvest: spring, fall

Wild garlic is a strong and flavorful plant. Unmowed, the top growth reaches 12 to 18 inches tall, with hollow gray-green leaves emerging from a single bulb, roughly ½ inch in diameter. Wild garlic is non-native with a highly aggressive growth habit. You know what that means, right? Harvest to your heart's content!

Wild garlic may grow in clumps or as individual plants. The two growth habits are typical of different growing conditions. You'll find the clumps in lawns. These plants have smaller bulbs, and slim, tender foliage that looks a lot like grass, only slightly darker. Because it grows faster than grass, you may notice patches in your lawn that are taller than the rest. Pick a stem and see if it smells like onion or garlic. The scent is an important identification characteristic: All alliums smell like onions or garlic.

In shady, wooded areas you'll find wild garlic growing as individual plants or in small clumps of just a few bulbs. This habitat makes for easier, more productive harvesting because the plants (and their bulbs) are larger overall. Also, because the bulbs grow singly, they're easier to clean. However, the foliage of these plants is tougher than the foliage of the clumped wild garlic, and therefore less useful as an herb. They can still be used as a bouquet garni to flavor a broth but should be removed before serving.

Wild garlic flowers are edible, tasty, and pretty, with pink or purple petals.

bulbils

Wild garlic sometimes produces flowers and bulbils at the same time.

Wild garlic often forms bulbils instead of flowers, and sometimes it produces both at the same time. Each bulbil is a pop of garlicky flavor, and they look like something out of Dr. Seuss. Small and purple, each bulbil sprouts a stem, making the cluster look like a wild hairdo. When the sprouted bulbils fall to the ground, they take root and there you have it, the circle of life.

HARVESTING

The best time to harvest wild garlic is in spring, when the bulbs are plump and full. By midsummer, the leaves may have gone dormant, making them difficult to locate. Also, the foliage will have drawn on the stored nutrition in the bulbs, leaving them less plump and tasty. To harvest the bulbs, grasp the stems as close to the soil as possible and pull straight up. If you're harvesting a clump, you'll see that the small bulbs hold a lot of dirt.

Any time you harvest the roots of a plant, you're reducing the plant population. However, wild garlic is considered invasive in many states, and since it grows in great abundance this isn't usually an issue. Still, it's a good idea to leave a few plants behind for next year.

CLOSE COUSINS

Wild onion (*Allium canadense*) is a close relative, but it has solid leaves and a distinctive netted sheath covering the bulb. Nodding onion (*A. cernuum*) is a showier cousin with larger, nodding flowers that some people (like me!) include in their gardens. Both wild onion and nodding onion are native to the United States and can be used in the same way as wild garlic.

wild onion (*A. canadense*)

nodding onion (*A. cernuum*)

FEASTING

I consider the flavor of wild garlic equal to that of ramps (*A. tricoccum*), which is a far less plentiful, sometimes endangered member of the onion family.

Leaves and stems. Tender young wild garlic foliage can be chopped and used like chives, but older leaves and stems can be too tough to chew. Use them to flavor a soup or stew, then remove the tough leaves.

Bulbs. Wild garlic bulbs make an excellent garlic substitute. The bulbs are smaller than those of cultivated garlic, and they require some cleaning. Cut off the stems and swish the bulbs in a bowl of water to remove most of the dirt. Slice off the end of the bulb with the small rootlets, then continue to clean in changes of water until all the dirt is gone.

You can use the bulbs fresh, or you can dry them at 95°F (35°C) for future use. Dried wild garlic bulbs can be rehydrated or ground into wild garlic powder. Use pickled bulbs as a cocktail garnish.

Flowers and bulbils. Wild garlic flowers make a tasty garnish, and the bulbils can be used as you would use the bulbs. Since the bulbils are even smaller than the underground bulbs, you'll probably want to use them whole, or infuse them in oil or vinegar (page 235) to make a flavored salad dressing.

WHERE AND HOW TO FIND

- Very common in lawns, parks, open fields, and dappled woods
- Perennial bulb that will return to the same spot year after year
- Goes dormant in summer, so look in spring and sometimes again in fall
- Grows in both sun and shade
- Grows in clumps in lawns and individual plants in wooded areas

At this stage of growth, harvest the bulbils to use fresh or dried.

ID CHECKLIST

- Wild garlic isn't always easy to spot, but once you know what it looks like, you'll see it everywhere.

- Foliage looks a lot like grass in sunny spots, although it's usually a slightly darker green.

- Leaves and stems have a gray-green color when growing in shade.

- Stems are hollow.

- Stems have a strong garlic smell when crushed.

- Stems have one or two leaves, attached low on the stem.

- Plants seldom flower, but often produce pink or purple bulbils, which might look like flowers from a distance.

- Plants sometimes produce flowers and bulbils simultaneously.

- Germinated bulbils look like a big, poufy hairdo in spring.

germinated bulbils

CHAPTER 2

GREEN WEEDS

of Sunny, Disturbed Soil

These plants are most common
where the ground has been disturbed,
either from construction, agriculture,
or erosion. You may also find them
in gardens, parking lots, playgrounds,
and city parks.

EVENING PRIMROSE

Oenothera biennis

A.k.a.: sundrop, evening star

Best part to eat: root

When to harvest: spring and fall

While there are several species of evening primrose, *Oenothera biennis* is the most delicious. This biennial plant forms a rosette of foliage close to the ground in its first year. Leaves have a distinctive, prominent vein down the center, which is either white or tinged with pink. In its second year, the plant produces a stem that can grow to be over 5 feet tall. Yellow flowers march up the bloom stalk.

The roots, leaves, and flowers of evening primrose are all edible, but I consider the roots to be the only part really worth harvesting. The flowers are mostly decorative, with a mild, sweet flavor. The leaves are nothing to write home about, but they'll fill out a stir-fry or quiche if you need to supplement your greens. The flower stalks can be peeled and eaten raw or cooked, before the flowers open.

FEASTING

Roots. Many accounts describe evening primrose root as having a strong peppery flavor, but I disagree. Maybe the people who say that harvested the root out of season. Evening primrose roots are best harvested in the fall of the plant's first year or in early spring of its second year, before the tall stem begins to grow. I find the flavor mild and appealing, with just a hint of black pepper.

Evening primrose root should be peeled. It can then be sliced and cooked in soups and stews, or boiled, roasted, or mashed, and served as a vegetable. Some foraging friends report that eating evening primrose root raw causes an itchy feeling in the back of the throat. Since the raw root can be fibrous and tough, save yourself the possibility of unpleasant itching and don't eat it raw!

Leaves. The foliage of evening primrose is also described as having a peppery flavor, and perhaps this is true later in the growing season. But in early spring, the foliage is not particularly spicy. After you've finished chewing, you may notice a slightly spicy, not unpleasant aftertaste. If you're not sure where you stand on the spicy food spectrum, try adding a few leaves, chopped, to a stir-fry and see where that gets you.

Harvest evening primrose roots at the end of their first year or beginning of their second, before the plant produces flowers.

Flowers. These make a very attractive and mild salad ingredient or garnish, and flower stalks can be peeled and eaten if you don't mind sacrificing the blooms.

Seeds. The seeds of evening primrose are edible, and some people appreciate their medicinal properties. I don't bother with them because I'm all about the food, and the seeds have no appreciable flavor.

OTHER SPECIES

There are many species of *Oenothera*, some perennial, some biennial, some with yellow flowers, some with white or pink flowers, some with multiple edible parts, and some that are not considered edible at all. All parts of *O. biennis* can be eaten, and it is the most widely distributed species in the United States. *O. villosa*, *O. clelandii*, and *O. oakesiana* are also edible, although perhaps not as delicious. I have never tasted them, but that's the general opinion among foragers.

O. villosa

EVENING PRIMROSE
KNOW BEFORE YOU EAT

WHERE AND HOW TO FIND

- Biennial plant that reseeds itself
- Can often be found in large colonies
- Grows best in full sun (open fields, parks, roadsides)
- Spotted most easily in summer when flower stalks stand tall

- Tolerates a range of soils
- Adapts to both moist and dry growing conditions
- Remains standing over winter
- Tall dried stalks are an indicator for where to look for next season's first-year foliage

ID CHECKLIST

- First-year growth is a basal rosette of foliage; outer ring of leaves lies flat against the ground.

- Lance-shaped (lanceolate) leaves, 2–7 inches long, may be toothed or have wavy margins.

- Leaves have prominent midrib.

- Second-year growth includes a hairy stem that produces large yellow flowers, approximately 2 inches in diameter.

- Foliage along the flower stalk is arranged alternately.

- Flowers have four petals and open in the evening (hence the name), usually closing by morning; they may remain open on a cloudy day.

- Mature plants may be 1–6 feet tall.

- Second-year stem may be reddish, white leaf midribs may have a pink flush, and the top of the edible root is often reddish.

basal rosette laying flat

lance-shaped leaf

flower stalk

four-petaled flowers

LAMB'S QUARTERS
Chenopodium species

A.k.a.: wild spinach, goosefoot, fat hen, pigweed

Best part to eat: leaves and stems

When to harvest: before flowering

Lamb's quarters is cultivated as a vegetable in Asia and parts of Africa. In Europe and the Americas, it's considered an annoying weed. Go figure. There are several species of lamb's quarters that are very similar in both flavor and appearance: *Chenopodium album*, *C. berlandieri*, and *C. fremontii*. All three can be used in the same way.

Lamb's quarters may be anywhere from one to several feet tall, depending on the growing conditions. Its most obvious identification characteristic is the white mealy covering, which makes the youngest leaves look powdery or dusty on top. Foliage is vaguely diamond or triangle shaped, reminiscent to some of a goose foot, which gives the plant one of its common names.

Once it has set seed, the plant dies quickly, so if you want to prolong your harvest, pinch off the top 6 to 8 inches of stem every week. This will prevent the plant from setting seed and will keep it producing tender, tasty greens.

Lamb's quarters is an excellent cut-and-come-again wild crop.

FEASTING

Like many other members of the beet and spinach family, lamb's quarters contains oxalic acid, and shouldn't be eaten raw in great quantities. Oxalic acid can interfere with the absorption of calcium and may aggravate arthritis, gout, or kidney stones, but only if eaten in large amounts.

Cooking breaks down the oxalic acid, making it safe to eat. And since lamb's quarters tastes better cooked than raw, that's just fine. It's also a healthy little green, high in vitamins A, B, and C as well as beta-carotene, antioxidants, and several minerals.

Like spinach, lamb's quarters reduces significantly in volume when cooked, so you'll want to harvest more than you think you need. Unlike spinach, lamb's quarters is tender and tasty all summer long, not just in cool weather.

Leaves. The leaves of lamb's quarters have a mild flavor and can be used any way you'd use spinach: in soups, egg dishes, casseroles, spring rolls, pasta filling, and pitas. Combine lamb's quarters with strongly flavored greens to make a balanced greens dish.

Stems. The tender, flexible stem tips of lamb's quarters are tasty served with a little sesame oil and lemon juice. You may hear foragers talk about using tender shoots of many young plants as they would asparagus, but that doesn't mean the plants taste like asparagus. It simply means they can be treated and prepared the same way you might asparagus.

You can feel the right place to cut the stems of the lamb's quarters by flexing them back and forth. In mid- to late summer this will give you pieces about 8 inches long and between ¼ to ½ inch thick. If the stem doesn't bend easily where you are trying to flex it, it's too tough and you need to move up the stem to younger plant tissue.

Young stems harvested in early summer can be steamed or microwaved, but by the end of July, you'll probably want to boil them. The stems of lamb's quarters are more fibrous than asparagus, and boiling produces a more tender vegetable than steaming.

Seeds. While many foragers appreciate lamb's quarters leaves, some hardcore foragers also harvest the seeds. Quinoa (C. *quinoa*) is a close cousin of lamb's quarters, although lamb's quarters seeds are significantly smaller than quinoa seeds.

Lamb's quarters seeds require a lot of processing. Not only are they surrounded by a dry husk that is fibrous and not tasty, but they also contain saponins, which give the seeds a bitter flavor. Harvest mature seeds after the foliage has turned brown. You'll need to rub off the chaff, winnow the seeds, soak them in water for 24 hours, then rinse the seeds in fresh water. The processed seeds can be dried and ground into flour, or sprouted and added to salads and sandwiches. You can decide for yourself if it's worth the work!

unripe lamb's quarters seeds

WHERE AND HOW TO FIND

- Needs a little warmth to start them growing; check when spring begins to feel like summer
- Grows in sunny garden beds and along the edges of neglected spaces like playgrounds, parks, and fields
- Grows well in disturbed soils
- Easiest to spot in late summer when tall, and when plumes of seeds are obvious, but this is not the best time to harvest
- Annual plant that reseeds itself
- Grows in same spot year after year
- Grows in every state
- Tolerates a wide range of climates and soils

ID CHECKLIST

- Herbaceous annual grows to be 3–5 feet tall at maturity.
- Mature leaves are arranged alternately on the stem of the plant (first few pairs of leaves may be arranged opposite each other).
- Leaves have wavy or jagged edges; young leaves may have smooth edges at first.
- A whitish covering on new foliage fades with time.
- The undersides of leaves are white.

- Grooved stems may be striped with red or purple variegation.
- Seeds are held in clusters, enclosed in dried, brown chaff.
- Mature seeds are black or very dark brown.

Leaves alternate on stem.

Leaves have whitish covering.

common mallow

MALLOW

Malva species

A.k.a.: cheeseweed, cheese plant, buttonweed

Best parts to eat: fruits, leaves

When to harvest: summer, fall (fruits), any time (leaves)

little mallow

tall mallow

All mallow plants have five-petaled flowers followed by fruits that look like wheels of cheese, hence the common name cheeseweed. At the base of each fruit is a five-part collar called a calyx. A calyx is composed of sepals, which form a layer exterior to petals on some plants.

Several species of mallow make good edible greens. Common mallow (*Malva neglecta*), little mallow (*M. parviflora*), and tall mallow (*M. sylvestris*) can all be used in the same ways. The biggest differences among the species are the size of the leaves, the height of the plant, and the color of the flowers.

The foliage is generally roundish and may have toothed leaf margins, or rounded, almost scalloped edges. To my eye, the foliage closely resembles that of geraniums, although the two plants aren't closely related.

Common mallow (*M. neglecta*) has leaves 1/2 to 1 1/2 inch in diameter. The plant is low-growing with a spreading or creeping growth habit. It may get to be 1 to 2 feet tall, depending on growing conditions. Flowers are white, pale pink, or pale lavender.

Little mallow (*M. parviflora*) looks very similar to common mallow but its flower petals are slightly longer and the fruit is more wrinkled. Plants may grow slightly taller than common mallow with a more upright growth habit. Flower colors are similar to those of common mallow.

Tall mallow (*M. sylvestris*) has larger leaves (2 to 4 inches in diameter) and larger flowers than common mallow and little mallow. The plant may grow to be 2 to 4 feet tall, and its flowers are a bright pink.

Mallows have taproots, which make the plants drought tolerant and allow them to grow in generally inhospitable spots. There is some debate about whether mallows are annuals, biennials, or short-lived perennials. To me this indicates that they are not true annuals, because true annuals die back after producing seed. Depending on where you forage and how harsh the winters are, you may find mallows living more than 1 year. Even if mallows grow as annuals where you live, because they self-seed you're likely to find them in the same general area year after year.

FEASTING

Leaves. Mallows have a mild flavor. Combine them with bitter greens in stir-fries and egg dishes, or sauté them and serve as a side dish. While mallow leaves can be eaten raw, I don't enjoy them that way. The foliage is fuzzy and mucilaginous, and cooking the greens tempers both of these characteristics. Mallows are a respected cooking green in the Mediterranean and Middle East. Most Mediterranean recipes combine mallow greens with garlic, olive oil, and lemon juice. The leaves stay tasty all season long, unlike some greens that turn bitter in the heat of summer.

Mallow is in the same plant family as okra, and mallow's mucilage can be useful in the same way okra's is useful, namely to thicken soups, stews, and sauces. Larger mallow leaves can be blanched for 1 to 2 minutes and used instead of grape leaves to make dolmathes.

Flowers. Fresh mallow flowers can be added to salads. Because they are less mucilaginous than the leaves (and not hairy!) they are pleasant to eat raw.

Fruits. Mallow "cheeses" (fruits) can be eaten raw as a trail snack, or added to salads. They can also be boiled in water and added to mixed vegetables, or the boiled cheeses can be puréed in a blender with chickpeas and tahini to make a unique hummus.

If you do boil the cheeses, you can save the liquid, which is similar in consistency to egg whites, to use in a dessert application. Just be sure to remove the bracts that surround each individual cheese before boiling them. It's tedious and time consuming, but the bracts have a vegetal flavor that, while not unpleasant, is also not very dessert-ish. The mallow liquid can be whipped and used as meringue, but the whipped liquid isn't super stable. The addition of a single beaten egg white and cream of tartar helps mallow meringue hold its shape.

WHERE AND HOW TO FIND

- Emerges in spring, but really takes off when the weather warms up
- Look for flowers and fruits (a.k.a. cheeses) from early to late summer.
- Grows best in full sun but will tolerate some shade
- Shady spots produce larger, more tender leaves and fewer flowers and fruits.
- Highly drought tolerant and can be found in very dry growing conditions
- Likes disturbed soils
- Grows in playgrounds, garden beds, and parks—just about everywhere

ID CHECKLIST

- Herbaceous plant with hairy stems and leaves
- Leaves are held on long stalks.
- Leaf edges are toothed or scalloped.
- Flowers have five petals.
- Flowers are white, pale pink, pale purple, or bright pink.
- Fruits are held in calyx (looks like a collar).

scalloped leaves

toothed leaves

fruit and calyx

Melilotus officinalis

Melilotus alba

MELILOT

Melilotus officinalis, M. alba

A.k.a.: sweet clover, honey clover, yellow sweet clover, white sweet clover

Best part to eat: flowers (leaves are also edible but slightly less flavorful)

When to harvest: any time

Don't be fooled by the alternate common name of this plant. It is not the low-growing clover you find in your lawn with round pink or white flowers. This is a tough, drought-tolerant plant that can grow to be 4 feet tall. It's a common roadside weed that thrives in sunny, neglected spaces. *Melilotus officinalis* has yellow flowers and *M. albus* has white flowers. There is some question as to whether these are actually two separate species or varieties of the same species. I happily use both and find the flavors to be identical.

A member of the pea family, melilot has the three-lobed leaf shape typical of legumes. Both the foliage and flowers have a sweet, vanilla fragrance with overtones of hay. It's considered invasive in most parts of the United States and often appears in giant swaths, which means you can forage for this herb to your heart's content.

Young melilot plants that are not in bloom may be confused with alfalfa, which is edible in small quantities, but does not have the same flavor. Since flowers are an important identification characteristic for any plant, you might want to get to know melilot by harvesting when it's in bloom.

field of *M. officinalis*

Handle with Care

Melilot contains coumarin, which is responsible for the sweet hay scent we find in plants such as sweet woodruff, cinnamon, and cassia cinnamon. (Coumarin is also present in strawberries, apricots, and cherries.) When melilot gets moldy, the coumarin converts to dicumarol, which is an anticoagulant. Please don't be alarmed. It is only when certain fungi interact with the coumarin, converting it to dicumarol, that consumption may be dangerous. So dry your melilot carefully, and if you see any signs of mold on the plant, throw it away. It's that simple.

FEASTING

Melilot flowers and leaves can be used fresh or dried, but the flavor is intensified by drying. Some foragers think the fresh herb is bitter, but I disagree. I've used fresh melilot to make syrups (page 234) and have been very pleased with the flavor; it's slightly more delicate than that of the dried herb.

If you have a dehydrator, strip the leaves and flowers from their stems, lay them out in single layers on the shelves of your dehydrator, and dry them at 95°F (35°C) until they are crispy. If you don't have a dehydrator, use an elastic band to make bundles of the melilot stems and hang them someplace out of direct sun to dry. Once dried, strip the leaves and flowers from the stems. The dried herb should be stored in airtight containers out of direct sunlight.

Melilot can be used in place of vanilla or tarragon. Its flavor is slightly less sweet than vanilla, but it makes a good vanilla extract substitute when macerated in vodka or brandy. It also infuses well in cream (page 240) for a panna cotta or pudding, and melilot simple syrup makes an excellent cocktail ingredient.

Try substituting melilot for tarragon in savory dishes. It doesn't have exactly the same flavor profile, but it works well in recipes that traditionally call for tarragon. I use it with chicken, pork, and fish, as well as in fruit chutneys and pickles. It also makes an excellent salad dressing ingredient.

KNOW BEFORE YOU EAT

WHERE AND HOW TO FIND

- Grows everywhere (yes, even Antarctica)
- Look in sunny, neglected spaces like playgrounds, parks, and along the edges of fields and woods.
- Grows in moist soils
- May be very lush under good growing conditions
- Emerges in spring
- Easiest to spot in midsummer when flowers are in full bloom
- Harvest flowers and foliage at any time, as long as no mildew or fungus is present.

ID CHECKLIST

- Both *M. officinalis* and *M. alba* are herbaceous biennials.
- Deep taproot makes it drought tolerant.
- Leaves have three parts, medium blue-green on top and pale green underneath, and are arranged alternately on the stem.
- Leaf margins have small teeth.
- Stems are smooth when young. With maturity stems may branch and become grooved or ridged.
- Long narrow clusters of white or yellow flowers open from the bottom of the cluster up.
- Individual flowers are approximately ¼ inch long, and flower clusters are 2–6 inches long.
- Flower stalks emerge from where the leaf joins the stem (the leaf axil).
- Mature specimens may grow to be 2–4 feet tall.

flower stalks

toothed leaves

MILKWEED

Asclepias syriaca, A. speciosa

A.k.a.: common milkweed, showy milkweed, silkweed, butterfly flower

Best parts to eat: young stems, immature flower buds, flowers, young seed pods

When to harvest: early spring (young stems), late spring to early summer (immature flower buds), late spring to summer (flowers), summer (young seed pods)

There's a lot of misinformation out there about milkweed. Some people swear it's bitter; others claim it's poisonous. Neither is true. When properly harvested and prepared, milkweed is tender, delicious, and versatile. If I had to choose just one wild plant to eat, it would probably be milkweed. That's how good it is.

HARVESTING

Stems. Harvest young milkweed stems when they're 6 to 8 inches tall. They should be tender enough to snap by hand (just be sure to wear gloves if you don't want the plant's sticky white latex all over you; I've also read the latex can cause a rash, but I've never met anyone who has experienced this). Sometimes the top several inches of older stems are tender enough to eat. If you can easily break off the top of the stem with your hand, by all means do so. If you have to cut the stem, it's probably too fibrous to be tasty.

immature flower buds

Leaves. The mature leaves of milkweed can be bitter and should be removed from the shoots before cooking.

Buds. Young milkweed flower buds look like mini broccoli florets. They're held between two small, immature leaves, which are fine to include in your harvest. For savory dishes, harvest buds until they show a blush of pink.

Flowers. Gather mature milkweed flowers when they are freshly opened and fully pink. Shake off any insects that hitchhiked in on your harvest, but don't rinse the flowers. That would wash away the pollen and nectar, which is where the flavor comes from.

Pods. Immature milkweed pods are tasty and tender until they're 1½ to 2 inches long. They should be firm and plump, and entirely white inside. Split open a pod and if you see brown seeds among the silk, the pod is too mature for eating.

immature milkweed pod

FEASTING

Milkweed should always be eaten cooked, not raw. Boil or blanch (for 1 to 2 minutes) the shoots, flower buds, and pods, then cook them to completion in any number of ways: roasting, sautéing, or deep-frying. You may read that milkweed requires boiling in three changes of water, but this is not true. I bet the person who started that rumor harvested dogbane instead of milkweed.

The green parts of milkweed (shoots, unripe flower buds, pods) taste a little like green beans, only better. Serve them as a vegetable, in egg dishes, casseroles, and stews.

Mature milkweed flowers have a sweet, strongly floral scent and flavor. Milkweed flower syrup (page 234) makes a delicate sorbet and a unique cocktail ingredient. Milkweed pollen contains natural yeasts that can be used to make a naturally fermented milkweed cordial.

You may read that the white, immature silk inside milkweed pods tastes like cheese. I'm here to manage your expectations. It does not taste like cheese. It's vaguely sweet and *almost* melts with cooking. But no way is it cheesy. My favorite way to eat them? Battered and deep fried.

KNOW BEFORE YOU EAT

WHERE AND HOW TO FIND

- Grows best in full sun
- Found in neglected spaces and well-drained soils and where woods meet fields
- Grows in playgrounds, parks, and garden beds
- Easiest to spot in fall, when seed pods burst open and spill white fluff
- Check back in early spring for young shoots, and for each subsequent harvest.

ID CHECKLIST

- Plants have a large taproot.
- Stems are hollow.
- Stems don't branch.
- Leaves are oblong or oval with white or pink midrib, arranged opposite each other on the stem.
- Leaves are 2–5 inches long.
- Mature plants grow up to 4 feet tall.
- Immature flower buds look like broccoli florets.
- Mature flowers are pink, with five petals arranged in a star shape.
- Seeds are held in canoe-shaped pods.
- Brown seeds are attached to white fluff.

These milkweed buds are at the perfect stage for harvesting.

milkweed flowers

POISONOUS LOOK-ALIKE

Reports of milkweed's bitterness and toxicity are most likely the result of people mistaking dogbane (*Apocynum cannabinum*) for milkweed. Dogbane is a bitter plant that superficially resembles milkweed. Additionally, the two plants often grow side by side, so if you're not paying attention, you might inadvertently include some dogbane in your milkweed harvest. It's pretty easy to differentiate between the two once you know what to look for.

dogbane

PLANT PART	MILKWEED	DOGBANE
STEMS	hollow, non-branching	solid, branching
FLOWERS	pink, 5 curved-back petals in a star shape	white, 5-petaled, never fully open to star shape

ORACHE

Atriplex hortensis

A.k.a.: mountain spinach, saltbush, French spinach, orach, arrach

Best part to eat: leaves

When to harvest: before the plant flowers

Orache closely resembles its cousin, lamb's quarters. It can be a challenge to tell them apart, especially when the plants are young. Fortunately both are edible and both are tasty, so there's no worry about making a dangerous culinary error here.

Generally speaking, the foliage of orache emerges earlier than that of lamb's quarters. Both plants may have a white, mealy covering, especially on younger leaves. And both plants have foliage held in opposite pairs on the lower part of the plant. Young orache leaves are often held vertically, almost parallel to the stem, whereas lamb's quarters leaves are held flat, at an approximately 90-degree angle from the main stem. Additionally, the leaf base of orache foliage is either straight across the bottom, or has two downward-facing lobes that make it look like an arrowhead. The leaf base of lamb's quarters turns up rather than down or straight.

leaf base of orache

leaf base of lamb's quarters

In the United States orache is more common in the West than in the East, probably due to soil being more alkaline in the west. It tolerates high alkaline and high saline soils, and its leaves are known to excrete excess salt. As a result, orache foliage has a salty flavor, which varies in intensity depending on the soil where the plant grows. Red-leaved and yellow-leaved varieties are grown as cultivated garden vegetables.

wild orache

cultivated red orache

COUSINS

Some people think orache leaves resemble those of black nightshade (*Solanum nigrum*; edible) and datura (*Datura* spp.; not edible). I disagree. Both black nightshade and datura have larger, darker green leaves, and are larger plants with wider, more freely branching shapes and much larger, very different-looking flowers and fruits. Neither one produces foliage with a white, mealy coloring.

black nightshade

black nightshade fruit

datura

datura fruit

HARVESTING

Some people consider orache to be a warm-season green because, unlike spinach and lettuce, it doesn't bolt (go to seed) as soon as the weather gets warm. For that reason, you can harvest orache long after the lettuce and spinach season has passed. However, the most tender and tasty orache leaves are harvested in cool spring and fall weather.

If you visit your orache spot on a regular basis and pinch off the last 4 to 6 inches of the plant every few weeks, you'll be able to harvest young, tender leaves all summer long. Be sure to let at least one plant go to seed, so you'll be able to harvest again next year. Orache is a reliable self-seeder.

FEASTING

Leaves. Orache is often used as a spinach substitute. You can use orache greens any way you'd use spinach, but be sure to taste a few leaves before cooking. You want to know how salty the greens are to begin with, so you don't oversalt when cooking.

Like spinach, orache leaves reduce greatly in volume when cooked. You can prepare orache simply, sautéed in olive oil with a little garlic and lemon juice. Or you can add it to casseroles, soups, stews, and pasta dishes. While orache is edible raw, I think it tastes better cooked.

Like spinach, sweet potatoes, and Swiss chard, orache contains oxalates. If you have a history of kidney stones or gout, go easy on the orache just as you would with spinach or chard.

Seeds. The seeds of orache (like the seeds of lamb's quarters) contain saponins and should be soaked before using to remove their bitter flavor. While orache seeds can be dried and ground to use as flour, or added to soups and stews, they are small and require some work (drying, winnowing, soaking, drying again) to prepare. I put orache seeds in the category of famine food, unlike the greens, which are tasty any day of the week.

orache seeds

WHERE AND HOW TO FIND

- Tolerates highly alkaline and saline soils

- Is drought tolerant, but produces more lush, tender growth with regular water

- Found often on beaches and the edges of marshes

- Grows best in full sun but tolerates some shade

- Found in roadside ditches and abandoned spaces with good soil moisture

ID CHECKLIST

- An annual plant, it grows to 2–6 feet tall, depending on growing conditions.

- Gray-green or blue-green foliage has a white, mealy covering, especially on younger leaves.

- Lower leaves are arranged in opposite pairs and are often held in an almost vertical position in relation to the plant's stem.

- Leaves higher on the stem are arranged alternately.

- Foliage has a triangular or arrowhead shape, and may be 2–4 inches long.

- Stems are branching.

leaves arranged in opposite pairs

white, mealy covering on leaves

QUEEN ANNE'S LACE

Daucus carota

A.k.a.: wild carrot, bird's nest, bishop's lace

Best parts to eat: flowers, roots

When to harvest: in bloom (flowers), spring and fall (roots)

The queen has hairy legs. Repeat that until you couldn't forget it if you wanted to. Queen Anne's lace is a member of the carrot family, which includes a number of highly poisonous plants, so it's essential to understand how to safely identify it. Fortunately, it's easy.

First, check for a solid, hairy stem. The queen has hairy legs, but her poisonous look-alikes do not!

Second, look for old flower clusters that curve up and in upon themselves to form a bird's nest shape. Young Queen Anne's lace flowers are held in flat clusters. As they age, clusters form a bird's nest shape.

Finally, Queen Anne's lace flowers are surrounded by a collar of long (1 to 2 inches), branching bracts. Many clusters have a single dark bloom at the center. You can remember that by saying that Queen Anne pricked her finger while making lace and the dark flower is a drop of her blood. Or you could just remember it without the hokey story. You choose.

Three important identification characteristics are hairy stems (left), flower clusters that form a bird's nest as they age (top right), and branching bracts under the flowers (bottom right).

poison hemlock

water hemlock

 # POISONOUS LOOK-ALIKES

The two most common poisonous look-alikes for Queen Anne's lace are poison hemlock (*Conium maculatum*) and water hemlock (*Cicuta maculata*). Both hemlocks have hollow, smooth stems, while the stems of Queen Anne's lace are solid and hairy. Remember the queen.

Poison hemlock often grows much larger than Queen Anne's lace, reaching 6 to 9 feet tall. The stems of poison hemlock are splotched with purple and are often covered with a white bloom you can wipe away with your fingers. The

Remember, the queen has hairy legs! (They are also green with no splotches.)

Purple splotches on the stem are characteristic of poison hemlock.

flowers of poison hemlock are surrounded by much shorter bracts (about ¼ inch long) than the flowers of Queen Anne's lace.

Water hemlock usually grows in wet soils, and its foliage, while divided, is not feathery like the leaves of Queen Anne's lace. Additionally, its stems are often red or purple with prominent vertical veins.

Don't let fear keep you from experimenting with Queen Anne's lace, but do make sure all the identification characteristics that follow match up 100 percent.

FEASTING

Queen Anne's lace is a versatile wild edible with several tasty parts. The garden carrot (*Daucus carota* subspecies *sativa*) is very closely related to Queen Anne's lace: same genus, same species, different subspecies.

Roots. Queen Anne's lace is a biennial, and the best time to harvest its roots is between fall of the first year and spring of the second year. If harvested earlier, the roots may be too small to be worthwhile; later, the roots can be too woody to enjoy. Young roots may have a thin, woody core, but the cooked flesh can be scraped off to make a tasty mash. Older roots can be used as an aromatic in soups and stews but should be removed before serving.

Leaves. The foliage of Queen Anne's lace has a fresh, carrot flavor. You can use it instead of parsley as a garnish or in salads, or to make a tasty pesto.

Flowers. Queen Anne's lace jelly (page 238) is made from an infusion of the flowers, and it is often described as pink. Careful reading shows that most people who get the pink color add a strawberry or two, or a drop of food coloring. My jelly is pretty, but it's more orange than pink. The flavor reminds me of Juicy Fruit gum.

From Queen Anne's lace flowers you can also make a soda (page 232). The

roots

fruits

pollen contains yeasts that allow for natural fermentation.

Fruits. Flowers are followed by small green fruits, which dry to be brown with a mild, caraway flavor. These can be ground and used as a spice. Inside each fruit are two seeds, which have been used historically as birth control and as an abortifacient. Do not eat them if you are pregnant or trying to conceive.

KNOW BEFORE YOU EAT

WHERE AND HOW TO FIND

- Summer weed, although foliage may overwinter in warm climates
- Grows in sunny spots in playgrounds, parks, and fields
- Plants are easiest to spot in summer when in full bloom; harvest flowers and check back regularly for ripe seeds, then forage roots the following year.
- Biennial plant that reseeds itself; grows in the same spot year after year
- Grows in every state
- Tolerates a wide range of climates and soils

ID CHECKLIST

- An herbaceous biennial, it grows 3–4 feet tall at maturity.
- Foliage is feathery, with leaves arranged alternately on the stem of the plant.
- Stems are solid and hairy.
- First-year growth is a basal rosette of foliage only.
- Second-year growth produces a flower stem 2–4 feet tall.
- White, flexible taproot smells like carrot when broken or scraped.
- Flower clusters often have maroon or purple flowers at the center of the cluster.
- Dried flower heads curve in on themselves to form a bird's nest shape.

bird's nest seed head and long surrounding bracts

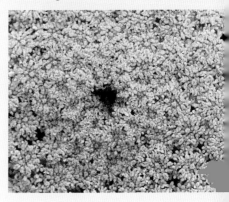

maroon spot in center

QUICKWEED

Galinsoga parviflora, G. quadriradiata

A.k.a.: gallant soldiers, potato weed, *guasca*, Peruvian daisy, galinsoga, shaggy soldier

Best part to eat: leaves

When to harvest: any time this plant is available, it's safe and tasty to harvest

Quickweed gets its common name from the fact that it germinates and grows very quickly. Both species produce thousands of seeds per plant and can grow from germination to ripening seed in less than 2 months, so it's not unusual to get several generations in a single growing season. No wonder quickweed is often available in large amounts.

These two quickweed species are very similar in appearance, though the stems and leaves of *Galinsoga quadriradiata* are hairier than those of *G. parviflora*. Both species can be used in the same way in the kitchen.

G. quadriradiata

G. parviflora

Farmers in the United States don't appreciate this common weed, although it's sold as an edible green in Latin America, where it's a native plant. Its shallow root system makes it easy to pull, but because it seeds so prolifically and grows so quickly, it can be challenging to get rid of. Fortunately, if you're a forager, you know what to do.

FEASTING

Some foragers dry the leaves and powder them to add to soups and stews, but I don't get much flavor from the dried greens. To get the most flavor and texture out of the plant, I either cook them fresh or blanch quickweed greens for 30 to 60 seconds, then freeze for later use.

Quickweed is a mild green and is especially useful combined with bitter greens in dishes like quiches, frittatas, and stir-fries. The application of heat brings out a slightly artichoke-ish flavor. That's not totally surprising, since both quickweed and artichokes are members of the daisy family.

The leaves of quickweed are either slightly hairy or pretty hairy, depending on which species you find. *G. quadriradiata* is hairy enough that I don't enjoy it raw, although *G. parviflora* makes a decent salad green. But since cooking improves both the flavor and the texture of the leaves, I prefer quickweed as a potherb.

Like many greens, quickweed reduces in volume when cooked, so pick two or three times more than you expect to need. Fortunately, it's tender and tasty all season long, even after flowering. Later in the season, harvest just the tips of the plant (4 to 6 inches) for tender greens.

Quickweed is an essential ingredient in ajiaco, a delicious Latin American soup, traditionally made with chicken and potatoes.

Coat buttons foliage has a creeping growth habit.

coat buttons flowers

coat buttons leaves

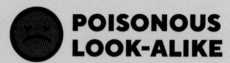 # POISONOUS LOOK-ALIKE

Some people think quickweed resembles coat buttons (*Tridax procumbens*), though I disagree. Now, I admit, the flowers of the two plants look very much alike. However, coat buttons has a recumbent growth habit, which means it creeps along the ground (only the flower stems are upright). Quickweed, however, has an upright habit. Additionally, the leaves of coat buttons are more triangular in shape and have rough, jagged leaf margins.

Some references list coat buttons as edible, and it has a long history as a medicinal herb, especially in India. So is it toxic? I don't know. But until I do, I'm not eating it and you shouldn't, either.

QUICKWEED
KNOW BEFORE YOU EAT

WHERE AND HOW TO FIND

- Grows best in full sun with regular moisture, but will tolerate shade
- Look in neglected spaces like parks, playgrounds, and garden beds.
- Easiest to identify in bloom
- Warm-weather weed
- Usually begins to flower in early summer

ID CHECKLIST

- This herbaceous annual plant has an upright growth habit.
- Plants grow to be approximately 2½ feet tall.
- Medium green leaves, with strongly impressed pattern of veins and toothed leaf margins, are arranged in opposite pairs on the stem.
- Leaves are slightly hairy to hairy, oval, with pointed tips.
- Leaves are 2–3 inches long.
- Stems are branching.
- Small white flowers (approximately ¼ inch in diameter) with yellow or gold centers appear on branching flower stems at the top of the plant.
- Flowers have five three-pointed petals (each one looks like three petals fused together).

leaves arranged in opposite pairs

five-petaled flowers

SOCHAN

Rudbeckia laciniata

A.k.a.: cutleaf coneflower, green-headed coneflower, tall coneflower

Best part to eat: leaves

When to harvest: spring and fall

Sochan is a widely distributed wild-flower in the United States and has been a much-loved garden perennial for years, but most people who grow it have no idea it also produces tasty leafy greens. In Native American communities, especially among the Cherokee, this is a much-loved edible plant. Like daylily greens, sochan foliage has a rich flavor.

Spring leaves are medium to dark green, ranging in diameter from 3 to 8 inches. The leaves have an interesting shape. Most are divided into three sections. The top section is the largest and is centered on the petiole. It is further divided into three lobed leaflets. Below and on either side are two more sections that are also deeply lobed. Early spring leaves have blunt or rounded tips, but as the plant grows, new leaves have pointier tips. Leaf petioles may be 4 to 8 inches long and are deeply grooved.

In summer sochan produces a flower stalk that grows to be 4 to 8 feet tall. Leaves are arranged alternately along the bottom part of the flower stalk, becoming smaller, with shorter petioles, as they climb. The uppermost leaves clasp the flower stalk directly. The top of the flower stalk is often bare, then branching to produce multiple flowers.

Sochan has an aggressive growth habit and spreads by underground rhizomes. You'll often find large clumps in rich soils with good moisture. As the plant grows, its lower leaves turn yellow and die back. When the plant finishes blooming, it puts out another round of tender, edible greens at ground level. Fall sochan leaves have a slightly stronger flavor than spring greens.

Sochan can be challenging to identify when young, but it's almost impossible to miss when it's in bloom. Look for bright yellow flowers with drooping petals surrounding a yellow-green center. This isn't the best time to harvest, but you can make a mental note of its location, then return in spring or fall to forage.

FEASTING

My favorite sochan greens are the teeny tiny, not-fully-unfurled leaves at the center of the plant. These can be cooked whole, leaves and petioles together. Spring leaves have a mild, nutty flavor, and while they're edible raw, I like them better cooked.

Slightly older spring leaves are also tender, and their petioles add a nice crunch to stir-fries and egg dishes; older petioles may need to be peeled to be palatable. While some people describe the fall flush of foliage as having a flavor like bok choy, I disagree. It's more flavorful than the milder spring greens, but doesn't have the mustard-family flavor that bok choy has.

LOOK-ALIKES

There are a few plants with foliage that resembles sochan, which is why identifying this plant in bloom is a really good idea. Virginia waterleaf (page 210) foliage is similar to sochan in shape but is often marked with subtle, white variegation.

More difficult to differentiate is the foliage of some members of the buttercup family, which tends to be bitter and mildly toxic. Because the flavor isn't pleasant you'll stop eating before you do serious damage if you've harvested the wrong plant. Look for the tall, dried stems of last year's flowers to make sure you've found sochan. Neither buttercup nor Virginia waterleaf produce tall flower stalks.

buttercup

WHERE AND HOW TO FIND

- Perennial plant forms large clumps
- Grows in sun or part shade
- Grows best in evenly moist, rich, well-drained soil
- Often found on stream and river banks
- Look for bright yellow flowers in summer to mark the growing spot.
- Last year's tall, dried flower stalks are a good identification characteristic.

ID CHECKLIST

- Spring growth is a basal rosette of foliage.
- Basal leaves are divided into three deeply lobed sections.
- Leaves are arranged alternately on flower stalk, getting progressively smaller as they grow up the stalk.
- Flower stalks are bare and branching near the top.
- Flowers have drooping yellow ray flowers (approximately 2 inches long) surrounding a yellow-green center.
- New flush of basal foliage growth emerges after the plant finishes blooming.

In spring the basal foliage of sochan is less finely lobed than later growth.

Sochan petals become more reflexed as the flower matures.

WHITETOP MUSTARD

Lepidium draba

A.k.a.: hoary cress (*Cardaria draba*)

Best part to eat: immature flower buds

When to harvest: any time the flower buds are tightly closed; before they start to show white

Whitetop mustard is a delicious, invasive, and not unattractive weed found in sunny, disturbed soils almost everywhere in the United States except the Southeast. The best edible part is the top several inches of the plant before the flowers fully open. This includes the unopened flower buds surrounded by a few leaves. At that time, it resembles its distant cousin, broccoli.

Whitetop spreads by a strong underground root system as well as by seed, and it's not unusual to see vast carpets of this plant in flower, when its white blooms make it stand out in the landscape. This isn't the time to harvest, but it's a good time to do some advance scouting for next year.

Whitetop is considered a serious agricultural weed and may affect the flavor of the milk from animals (goats, sheep, cows) that graze on it. You may see it listed as toxic to cattle, but this is in fact not true. Further research shows that some farmers actually train their cattle to eat whitetop to keep the plant under control. While farmers struggle with its eradication, foragers can enjoy its abundance.

FEASTING

Many mustards have a characteristic flavor reminiscent of horseradish. It's a strong flavor and you either love it or

These fully open flowers tell you the plant has passed the prime stage for eating.

you hate it. The strength of the flavor depends on the maturity of the plant and the species of mustard. Mature, fully flowering whitetop is too strong to suit my taste, but young whitetop, before the flowers open, is delicious. It has just the right amount of bite in the flavor to keep it interesting. Harvest when the flower buds are still tightly closed and green. It's fine to eat this plant if the buds are showing some white, but the flavor will be stronger and may require more boiling.

Since whitetop often grows in vast colonies, it's easy to harvest enough to both serve for supper and preserve for the future. Blanch your whitetop in boiling water for 1 to 2 minutes, then shock in ice water. You can either eat it fresh or let it dry and freeze for later use.

Because whitetop has a strong flavor, you may want to combine it with mild greens to use as a filling for pitas or stuffed pasta, or for quiches. It's also great in stir-fries, egg dishes, or served alone with the sauce of your choosing. I like a creamy sauce to balance the horseradish flavor of the greens.

The black seeds of whitetop can be used as a pepper substitute or can be ground into a mustard condiment.

CLOSE COUSINS

There are so many tasty mustards; I wish there were room in this book to describe all of them. Alas, there is not. But I'm going to sneak one more in here.

While whitetop is one of my favorite strongly flavored mustards, musk mustard (*Chorispora tenella*), also known as blue mustard, is one of my favorite mild mustards. The flowers of this mustard are purple or blue, and the plant is an annual, growing first in a basal rosette, which matures to a small plant about 12 inches tall. The flavor of musk mustard has only the vaguest resemblance to that of horseradish. It's slightly spicy, with a mushroomy, umami flavor. It makes an excellent salad green, or a savory filling for a tea sandwich. This is a mustard green I prefer to eat raw. The leaves have a lovely succulence and texture that disappears with the application of heat.

Musk mustard flowers make a pretty salad ingredient.

WHERE AND HOW TO FIND

- Easiest to identify when in bloom, but that is not the best time to eat
- Look in abandoned, sunny spots like parks, playgrounds, and fields.
- Harvest when the flower buds are still tightly closed and green.
- Perennial; grows in same spot every year

ID CHECKLIST

- Foliage is gray-green and covered with fine hairs.
- Leaves are widest near the base (lanceolate) and 1–4 inches long with toothed margins.
- Young leaves are arranged in a basal rosette.
- Leaves are arranged alternately on stem as flowering stem appears.
- Fully open, white flowers have a typical mustard shape: four petals arranged in an uneven cross with six stamens—two short, four long.
- Flowers are held in large, flat-topped clusters.
- Mature plants may be almost 2 feet tall when in bloom but should be harvested when younger.
- Flowers are followed by round or heart-shaped seed pods full of black seeds.

Note the four petals with six stamens: two short, four long.

This whitetop bud is at the perfect stage for eating.

CHAPTER 3

Sun-Loving TREES & SHRUBS

You may find these trees and shrubs growing in the wild, along neighborhood streets, and in city parks. Some people consider yucca to be a perennial and others call it a shrub. I've included it here because its structure feels more shrublike than perennial to me.

BLACK LOCUST, NEW MEXICO LOCUST

Robinia pseudoacacia, R. neomexicana

A.k.a.: false acacia, southwestern locust, pink locust, desert locust

Best part to eat: flowers

When to harvest: any time the flowers are in bloom

This is an easy tree to spot and identify, even from a car moving at 60 miles per hour. When locust trees are in bloom, you'll want to pull your car over and harvest, because these flowers don't last long! You'll see the ripe flowers in late spring or early summer (and sometimes another, smaller round of bloom in fall), and they last for about 2 weeks, depending on the weather. Hot weather makes the blooms pass more quickly than cool weather.

Robinia neomexicana is an understory tree native to the southwestern United States, while *R. pseudoacacia* is more common on the East Coast. On one website, the USDA lists black locust as native to all 48 of the lower states, but this is incorrect. Another USDA site explains that black locust has naturalized across the US. This is correct.

Cultivars of the New Mexico locust that are grown as street trees generally have bright, deep pink flowers and a single trunk. Trees in the wild are often multistemmed and have lighter pink flowers. Black locust is similar in its growth habit, albeit with white flowers instead of pink. Both trees have a suckering growth habit, producing new growth from underground rhizomes, which are modified stem tissue.

Locust trees are heavily armed, especially on the young branches, with most bearing pairs of sharp thorns at the base of each leaf. Some cultivars bred for landscaping may not have thorns.

Beware the thorns of the black locust and New Mexico locust! They protect the plant from herbivores . . . of which you are one.

FEASTING

Flowers. You'll find lots of recipes online for locust flower fritters. They're a tasty treat and a fun thing to do with kids, but you won't really get to appreciate the flavor or texture of the locust flowers this way. Honestly, what wouldn't taste good dipped in batter, deep fried, and sprinkled with powdered sugar?

Raw locust flowers make a great addition to salads and desserts. They have excellent substance and texture, and make a sweet, satisfying pop when you bite down on them. Sprinkle individual flowers on top of all kinds of salads (green, pasta, tuna, or chicken) or onto ice cream, cupcakes, or panna cotta. The flavor is floral, naturally sweet (but not overwhelmingly so), and also a little fruity.

Making a syrup with locust flowers (page 234) is a great way to capture the flavor and color of the blooms, and it can be used in different ways. I like it as a cocktail ingredient, but an even more impressive way to enjoy the syrup is as a base for sorbet. The addition of lemon juice turns the syrup from purple to magenta. It's as beautiful as it is delicious.

Pods and seeds. The pods and seeds are listed as toxic by some resources, while others list them as being a traditional food among Chiricahua Apache and Mescalero Apache peoples. Two well-respected fellow foragers, Sam Thayer and Arthur Haines, consider the seeds to be edible when cooked. Unripe green seeds are preferable, as dried brown seeds remain tough, even after soaking and boiling. I haven't yet experimented with the pods or seeds, but I trust Sam and Arthur. You can decide for yourselves whom to trust.

The white flowers of black locust taste just as good as the pink flowers of New Mexico locust.

LOOK-ALIKE

The honey locust tree (*Gleditsia triacanthos*) is sometimes confused with black locust, but it has several characteristics that make it easy to differentiate. First the honey locust is wickedly armed. Its thorns, rather than originating in pairs from the base of leaves, may emerge from the trunk or branches in long, multibranching clusters. They are seriously thorny: If you backed up into a honey locust thorn cluster you would be down for the count. Honey locust pods are two to four times longer than black locust pods, and often have a twisting shape. They are filled with an edible, sweet, green pulp. And finally, the flowers of honey locust are small, yellow-green, and not nearly as showy and beautiful as the flowers of black locust and New Mexico locust.

Top left: Honey locust flowers are small, yellow-green, and not showy. *Bottom left:* Honey locust pods have a twisting shape. *Right:* The thorns of the honey locust are wicked sharp.

black locust flowers

WHERE AND HOW TO FIND

- A popular street tree (especially the pink-flowered *R. neomexicana*), it is usually single stemmed.
- In the wild, this plant is often a multistemmed shrub.
- In nature, locust trees grow in part shade to full sun.
- As street trees, locusts tolerate full sun with adequate water.

ID CHECKLIST

- Mature trees of New Mexico locust are approximately 20–25 feet tall.
- Black locust trees grow to be 70–100 feet tall.
- Leaflets (½–2 inches long) are arranged alternately on stems to form a pinnate leaf.
- Foliage is blue-green to green in color and individual leaflets have smooth edges.
- The undersides of the foliage are a paler green than the tops of the leaves.
- Thorns are held in pairs at the base of most leaves, especially on young trees.

- Grapelike clusters of flowers, either pink or white, form in early summer.
- Typical pea-shaped flowers have individual blooms about 1 inch long.
- The white flowers of black locust have a yellow spot on the upper petal.
- Flowers are followed by bean-shaped pods with multiple small seeds.
- Seed pods of New Mexico locust are hairy.
- Both locust species sucker to form dense colonies of plants.
- Bark is deeply contoured, especially on older trees.

deeply contoured bark

pairs of thorns at leaf base

These black locust seed pods will ripen to be brown.

BRAMBLE BERRIES

Rubus species

A.k.a.: black raspberry / black cap, raspberry, wineberry, blackberry

Best part to eat: berries

When to harvest: The sequence is generally as follows: black cap, raspberry, blackberry, wineberry, running from late spring through fall

Bramble berries are some of the easiest and least intimidating wild edibles to forage because they look so familiar. Who doesn't recognize a raspberry?

Four of the most common bramble berries are black raspberries, raspberries, wineberries, and blackberries. These are also known as cane fruits, because the fruit grows on woody canes rather than vines or green stems. Brambles have perennial roots, so you'll find them in the same place year after year. But the canes are biennial. First-year canes produce leaves, and second-year canes produce fruit. After their second year, the canes die back, so wild bramble berry patches are always composed of a combination of first- and second-year canes.

The foliage of most bramble berries is compound, meaning each leaf is divided into three to seven leaflets. Second-year wineberry canes produce leaves with three leaflets.

Flowers of these bramble berries are white to pale pink with five petals each. Each flower has multiple pistils, and each pistil forms a fruit when pollinated. That's right, each bump on the berry is an individual fruit, which together form an aggregate.

When bramble berries are ripe, they practically fall off into your hands. The fruit ripens gradually, over a period of

The young, red calyces of wineberries are very pretty and are an excellent identification characteristic.

2 to 3 weeks, so it's worth checking your berry patches once a week to maximize your harvest.

FEASTING

Bramble berries are delicate fruits. They'll keep for a day or two in the refrigerator but can be preserved longer by freezing.

Wash the fruit by dunking it briefly in water, then drain the berries on a paper towel. (Washing the berries under running water may break the fruit.) When they're dry, spread the berries in a single layer on a cookie sheet covered with wax paper and freeze. When the fruit is frozen, transfer it to ziplock bags for long-term storage.

Bramble berries are delicious straight off the cane, but if you can resist eating them all while you pick, try them in jams, jellies (page 238), cobbler, pie, sorbet, ice cream (page 240), and booze (page 237).

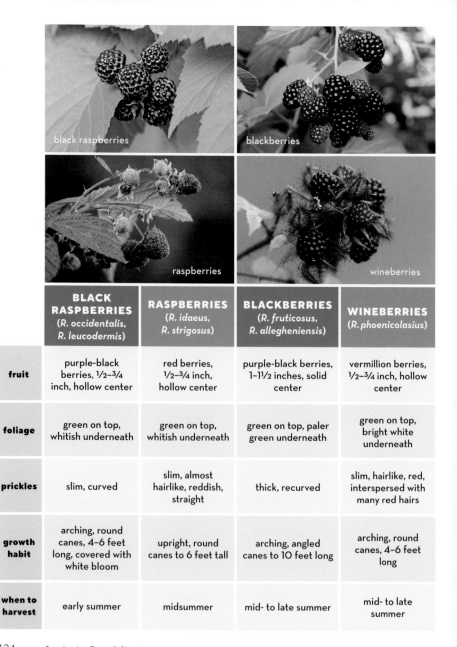

black raspberries

blackberries

raspberries

wineberries

	BLACK RASPBERRIES (*R. occidentalis, R. leucodermis*)	**RASPBERRIES** (*R. idaeus, R. strigosus*)	**BLACKBERRIES** (*R. fruticosus, R. allegheniensis*)	**WINEBERRIES** (*R. phoenicolasius*)
fruit	purple-black berries, 1/2–3/4 inch, hollow center	red berries, 1/2–3/4 inch, hollow center	purple-black berries, 1–1 1/2 inches, solid center	vermillion berries, 1/2–3/4 inch, hollow center
foliage	green on top, whitish underneath	green on top, whitish underneath	green on top, paler green underneath	green on top, bright white underneath
prickles	slim, curved	slim, almost hairlike, reddish, straight	thick, recurved	slim, hairlike, red, interspersed with many red hairs
growth habit	arching, round canes, 4–6 feet long, covered with white bloom	upright, round canes to 6 feet tall	arching, angled canes to 10 feet long	arching, round canes, 4–6 feet long
when to harvest	early summer	midsummer	mid- to late summer	mid- to late summer

WHERE AND HOW TO FIND

- Bramble berries are most prolific in full sun, although wineberries tolerate more shade than their cousins.

- Brambles are often edge species, so look for them where fields merge with woods.

- Blackberries and wineberries are often considered invasive and may form thickets in ditches and along roadsides.

ID CHECKLIST

- Raspberries have an upright growth habit.

- Black raspberries, wineberries, and blackberries have canes with an arching growth habit; these arching canes may root when their tips touch the ground.

- Stems are armed with prickles.

- Black raspberries and raspberries have a powdery, white coating on their canes; you can rub the coating off with your fingers.

- Bramble foliage is compound, with toothed leaf margins.

- The flowers of these four bramble berries are white or pale pink with five petals and numerous pistils in the center.

stem prickles

foliage

flowers

CHOKECHERRY

Prunus virginiana

A.k.a.: bird cherry, bitter berry, western chokecherry

Best part to eat: fruit

When to harvest: when fruit tastes pleasantly sour but not astringent (late summer to early fall)

Chokecherries flower sometime between April and June, depending on where you live. The plants stand out in the landscape when they're in bloom, so make note when you pass a good clump, and check back in late summer or early fall. Chokecherry fruit will be red in midsummer, but they usually take a month or more to fully ripen. Mature fruit may be dark red, purple, or black, depending on the variety. All ripe chokecherries can be used in the same ways. Underripe chokecherries are unpleasantly astringent, so until you know which color your chokecherries ripen to, don't assume they're ready! Taste a cherry or two before making a massive harvest.

These are highly adaptable plants, equally at home in rich or poor soil, along roadsides, in ravines, or on the edges of woods and streams. They often cluster along fence lines; birds sitting on the fence digest the fruit and expel the seeds. (That's a nice way of saying "poop out the seeds.")

Plain old chokecherries aren't often sold as landscape plants, but purple and red leaf cultivars have become popular. In the Rocky Mountains and Great Plains, where this fruit has always been appreciated, you can find the straight species for sale.

Some red chokecherries are ripe and some are not. Taste a sample before you harvest, to be sure they're not too astringent.

FEASTING

Historically in North America, Indigenous peoples dried whole chokecherries for long-term preservation. These would be ground into flour or used in pemmican (a paste of dried meat, fat, and other ingredients). Like other members of the rose family, the unprocessed seeds of the chokecherry contain cyanide compounds. But don't let this deter you from eating them. Boiling or drying makes the seeds safe to consume. If you're going to just use the fruit (for juice or jelly) you don't need to worry about this at all. And remember, we've all swallowed a few apple seeds (apples are another member of the rose family) and lived to tell the tale.

It's easy to avoid the pits entirely by juicing the fruit, then turning that juice into jelly (page 238), syrup (page 234), or wine (page 236). If you prefer jams to jellies, you can run the fruit through a food mill to remove the seeds. My favorite way to use chokecherries is to infuse them in rye whiskey (page 237). Then, because I don't like to waste food, I use the boozy fruit pulp to make a superb jam (she says modestly).

black cherry leaves and berries

LOOK-ALIKE

Black cherries (*Prunus serotina*) look similar to chokecherries and are also edible. Black cherries have darker green leaves, which are narrower in shape than chokecherries. Black cherries also have rounded teeth on their leaf margins, while chokecherries have pointed teeth. The fruit of both species is borne in clusters along a central stem. Each individual fruit attaches to the central stem with a short, thin stem. Chokecherries attach to their individual stems the same way store-bought sweet and sour cherries do. But the individual stems of black cherries end in a cup that holds the top of the fruit, sort of like the cap at the end of an eggplant. Finally, chokecherry trees are usually much smaller than black cherry trees; chokecherry trees are 20 to 30 feet tall whereas black cherry trees can grow to be 70 to 80 feet tall.

CHOKECHERRY
KNOW BEFORE YOU EAT

WHERE AND HOW TO FIND

- Grows best in full sun
- Tolerates some shade, but will not produce as many flowers or as much fruit
- Tolerates a wide range of soils but is not happy in clay
- Appreciates well-drained soil, and while drought tolerant once established, will thrive along river banks and streams

bottle-brush cluster

serrated leaf margins

ID CHECKLIST

- Small tree or multistemmed shrub grows to a mature height of 20–30 feet.

- Leaves are oval, 1–4 inches long, with sharply serrated margins.

- Foliage is dark green with paler undersides.

- Flowers are held in bottle-brush clusters approximately 3–4 inches long.

- Individual flowers are white, have five petals, and are about 1/2 inch in diameter.

- Fruit matures to red or black, depending on the variety.

- Each fruit contains a single, proportionately large seed.

- Tree bark is marked by horizontal pores (lenticels) that allow for gas exchange and are typical of cherries and plums.

- All cherries are susceptible to a specific fungus called black knot—it's black, hard, and grows to encircle branches and twigs. If you see this fungus growing on a tree, chances are it's a cherry (or a plum).

ripe black chokecherry leaves and berries

CRABAPPLE

Malus species

A.k.a.: crabtrees, crabs

Best part to eat: fruit

When to harvest: when ripe; summer, fall, or winter, depending on where you forage

Both crabapples and regular apples are members of the genus *Malus*. The primary difference between the two groups is fruit size. Any apple with a diameter smaller than 2 inches is considered a crabapple. Because they are so similar to regular apples, you can use crabapples in many of the same ways you'd use a regular apple, as long as you remember that they're not as sweet as most larger apples.

Crabapples are bred for looks, not taste, and the flavor varies widely from tree to tree. Most are extremely sour and many have a grainy texture. But some are as crisp and delicious as a full-size apple, and even those that don't have wonderful texture yield a tart juice you can use in jellies, cocktails, and frozen desserts.

Crabapples are a popular garden plant, and you'll find them in parks and at abandoned homesteads. Crabapple trees often form groves, as they send up new suckers from the tree roots. Birds and other animals do their share of planting when they eat the fruit and poop out the seeds.

Crabapples have loads of natural pectin, which explains why they're so sour. (Pectin is very sour.) The pectin level declines with time, so if you want to make a no-pectin-added jelly (page 238), harvest barely ripe or underripe fruit. Otherwise, let the crabapples stay on the tree to sweeten up a bit. Pick them before they start to shrivel. Crabapples are persistent fruit, which means they'll hang on the tree all winter long until birds and squirrels (and foragers) have eaten every last one.

Next time you pass a crabapple tree with ripe fruit, taste one. (As long as you have permission and you know the fruit hasn't been sprayed with anything toxic, of course.) Yes, it will be sour. But imagine that tartness tempered with a little sugar and a few spices. It's the reason why my pantry is full of crabapple juice, crabapple sauce, and crabapple syrup (page 234). And did I mention crabapple bourbon (page 237)? Cheers!

Crabapple flowers range from white to deep pink and everything in between.

Crabapples come in many sizes and colors.

FEASTING

I grew up thinking crabapples were poisonous. (I also grew up thinking life was fair and goodness would be rewarded, so go figure.) After all, I never saw anybody eat them, and why would people let all that pretty fruit go to waste if it was worth eating? Crabapples are extremely popular garden plants, but almost everyone grows them for their delicate spring flowers, not for their fruit.

I don't think there's a more versatile fruit on this planet. Larger crabapples (with a diameter of 1 to 2 inches), which tend to have better texture than smaller fruit, can be eaten raw or pickled. Smaller fruit may not be great for eating out of hand, but they still have plenty of culinary value. You can make homemade pectin to use for making jelly with low-pectin fruit (page 238), to make syrup (page 234) to use as a base for sorbet and ice cream, or to make crabapple wine (page 236) that is surprisingly reminiscent of port. Infuse a bottle of bourbon with crabapples (page 237) to make a classic fall cocktail. The combination of tart fruit and sweet whiskey is terrific.

Cooking obliterates any textural issues you might have with small crabapples, so use them in pies, cakes, applesauce, and fruit leather. You'll need to adjust the sugar if you're using a traditional apple recipe, since crabapples are almost always more sour than larger apples.

Oh, and one more thing! If you make your own cider, try adding a few crabapples to your next batch. It adds a little zip and zing, and balances out the sweetness of larger fruit.

WHERE AND HOW TO FIND

- One might ask, "Where can you *not* find crabapples?"
- This tree can be found in parks, fields, backyards, front yards . . . almost anywhere.
- Crabapples are full-sun trees, but animals don't usually consider this when they poop, so you may find crabapple trees growing in part shade.
- Crabapple trees in part shade won't produce as much fruit as trees in full sun.

ID CHECKLIST

- Crabapple trees grow to be 10–40 feet tall.
- The bark is grayish-brown, smooth when young, and displays vertical scales and cracks when older.
- Foliage is 1–4 inches long and arranged alternately on the branch.
- Leaves are usually elliptical and have serrated margins; some (not many) crabapples have lobed foliage.
- Flowers may be white, or innumerable shades of pink, and may be single (5 petals), semidouble (6–10 petals), or double (more than 10 petals).
- Crabapples look like mini apples.
- Fruit is ½–2 inches in diameter.
- Fruit may be yellow, orange, pink, or red and often persists on the tree throughout winter, unless some forager comes around and picks it all.

single, five-petaled crabapple flowers

These large crabapples are tart and crisp.

MAGNOLIA

Magnolia species

A.k.a.: bull bay, cucumber tree, umbrella tree, sweetbay

Best part to eat: flower buds, flowers

When to harvest: early spring and fall (flower buds), spring (flowers)

Very few people realize that both magnolia flowers and buds are edible. You now belong to a very exclusive club.

There are more than 200 species of magnolia, but not all are equally delicious. Fortunately, three of the most common, *Magnolia virginiana*, *M. grandiflora*, and *M. × soulangeana,* are all quite tasty. To me, the flowers of *M. stellata* are not very delicious, but they're safe to eat, so feel free to sample a petal or two to see if you like them.

Not surprisingly in a genus that has so many members, it's difficult to describe "the magnolia." All magnolias can be counted on to produce large, beautiful flowers, which are often quite fragrant. That fragrance translates to flavor, and the most flavorful magnolia flowers have warm, spicy notes. Many people compare the flavor to that of ginger, cardamom, and clove. They aren't far off, but please taste a few petals and make your own decision.

The bark of most magnolias is smooth and gray, and the height and form of various magnolia species are highly variable, ranging from 15 to over 100 feet tall, and including both multi-stemmed and single-trunked trees.

Magnolia leaves are used in cooking in some cultures. In Japan, the extra large leaves of *M. obovata* are used as wrappers or plates, much the way banana leaves are used in the tropics. The leaves of *M. virginiana* can be substituted for bay leaf (a related plant).

FEASTING

Flowers. Magnolia pickles are probably the most familiar (at least to foragers) way to use magnolia petals. While they're tasty, I prefer using my magnolia flowers in other ways. Why? Because to me, pickles taste more like the brine they're pickled in than the item being pickled. And I want to taste my foraged ingredient, not just vinegar. If you do pickle magnolia flowers, try serving them with a sharp cheddar. The flavor combination is terrific.

Taste a fresh magnolia petal straight off the tree to see if you like the flavor. The best are spicy and complex, and the worst taste a lot like dirt. Raw petals can be used in salads or as a flavorful garnish. I chop them into bite-size

M. × soulangeana **flowers are delicious.**

pieces for salads, since the flavor can be strong. As a garnish, they go especially well with chicken and pork.

The flavor of magnolia flowers infuses well in cream (page 240) and alcohol (page 237). You can use the whole flower for either of these preparations. I find the pistils and stamens (the reproductive parts of the flower) to be a little too thick to enjoy chewing on, but for a recipe where you plan to discard the solids, such as infusing cream for panna cotta or infusing bourbon for a very special mint julep, there's no reason not to use the entire bloom.

Buds. Magnolia buds can be harvested either in late fall or early spring, before they break dormancy. They're encased in a fuzzy covering. Use a microplane to grate the buds (fuzzy covering and all) and use as a spice in dry rubs,

These magnolia buds are at the right stage for harvesting.

marinades, pie fillings, and crisp toppings. Like the flowers, magnolia buds have a spicy flavor. You can preserve the buds for at least a year by drying them in a dehydrator at 95°F (35°C), keeping them in a glass jar with a tight-fitting lid, and storing them out of direct sun.

MAGNOLIA
KNOW BEFORE YOU EAT

WHERE AND HOW TO FIND

- Trees grow in full sun to part sun, but flower best in full sun.
- Plants require moderate moisture; you won't find them in the desert.
- While some people think of magnolias as growing in southern climates, many species are quite cold hardy.
- Mature trees can be found at abandoned homesteads, in city parks, as street trees, and in private yards (be sure you have permission to harvest).

M. virginiana   *M. grandiflora*

ID CHECKLIST

- Trees may be either evergreen or deciduous, depending on the species.
- Deciduous magnolias often flower before they leaf out, making them visually spectacular.
- Flower buds have fuzzy casings.
- Flowers may be white, yellow, pink, or purple, depending on the species or cultivar.
- Many species have large leaves.
- Leaves are generally elliptical in shape and arranged alternately on branches.
- Leaves of *M. virginiana* may be evergreen or deciduous, depending on the location; foliage is medium green on top, pale green to white underneath, and 3–6 inches long.
- Leaves of *M. grandiflora* are leathery and evergreen; shiny, dark-to-medium green on top, fuzzy, rust brown underneath, and 5–10 inches long.
- Leaves of *M.* x *soulangeana* are deciduous, medium green, often with noticeably pointed leaf tips; foliage is 3–6 inches long.

- Some species produce a cone-shaped fruit in late summer or early fall; seeds within the fruit ripen to a bright red color on most species.
- The jury is out on the edibility of the seeds, but at least one forager I trust says they taste terrible, so I'm not in a rush to experiment.
- Plants range from small, multistemmed trees topping off at 15 feet tall, to large, single-trunked specimens reaching more than 100 feet in height.
- Trees often branch low on the trunk.

fruit with seeds

OAK

Quercus species

A.k.a.: oaks

Best part to eat: acorns

When to harvest: fall or winter

Acorns are one of the most versatile wild foods you can harvest. They can be made into a gluten-free flour that adds richness to sweet and savory baked goods, or they can be eaten as nuts, mixed into burgers, or used as a soup base. They're an excellent source of starch and fat. You will never starve if you have acorns.

Almost everyone recognizes an oak tree. The characteristic lobed leaves make it easy to identify. White oaks have a reputation for the tastiest acorns, while red oak acorns generally require more work to make them palatable because of their higher tannin levels. Fortunately, as long as you have reliable taste buds, you don't need to know which kind of oak you've found.

HARVESTING

In the fall, look for the biggest acorns you can find, because the most labor intensive part of processing acorns is the shelling. If you can shell 50 large acorns to get the same amount of nut meat you'd get from 100 small acorns, you're ahead of the game. Collect your acorns after they've fallen from the trees, and discard any nuts that still have their caps attached or that have a small hole in them. A healthy nut will separate from its cap when it falls. A hole indicates the exit route of the oak weevil larva, which has been feeding on the nut all summer, so there probably isn't much deliciousness left inside. When the nuts fall to the ground in autumn, the larva chews its way out of the nut and pupates in the soil, emerging the following year as a full-grown weevil, which then lays its eggs inside a young (and impressionable) acorn.

Fall is a busy season for foragers, and since acorns are less perishable than many wild edibles, I often freeze them until I have more time to work in the kitchen. Freezing keeps the acorns

fresh, and also kills any weevil larvae that may have come along for the ride. The downside is that thawed acorns hold moisture, which makes them harder to shell. But you can remedy this by dehydrating them for a few hours before shelling. If you're going to make acorn flour, keep the dehydrator's temperature under 150°F (65°C) so as not to cook the starches in the nut. Those starches will help your acorn flour bind when you bake with it.

The first time I shelled acorns I placed a few nuts at a time between two dish towels and cracked them with a rubber mallet. Acorn shells are thin and easy to crack, but once you start to process acorns in greater numbers, consider getting a nutcracker.

FEASTING

Shelled acorns must be leached of their tannins before they can be eaten (see pages 141–42 for instructions). While several foraging friends swear that a sweet acorn exists, one that requires no leaching, I have never met this mythological acorn. Unleached acorns not only taste bitter, but consuming large amounts of tannins reduces the efficiency with which your intestines absorb nutrition. That's not a good thing.

So how will you leach your acorns? The answer depends on how you plan to use your nuts. If you're going to use your acorns as flour in baked goods, cold leaching is the way to go. Acorn flour has a rich flavor and is gluten-free. Since gluten is what helps baked goods rise and bind together, you'll often see recipes call for half acorn flour and half regular flour. Baked goods made with 100 percent acorn flour tend to be crumbly.

Hot leached acorns can be ground or chopped and used in baklava, falafel, as a coffee substitute, or as a rich soup base. And acorn syrup (page 234) makes an excellent cocktail ingredient.

acorn flour

How to Leach and Store Acorns

You can either hot leach or cold leach acorns. Cold leaching results in a more versatile end product, one that can be used as flour as well as in any way you'd use hot leached acorns. Cold leaching preserves the starches in acorns, which helps the flour bind. Remember, acorn flour contains no gluten, a protein that helps baked goods both rise and bind together.

HOT LEACHING

To hot leach acorns, fill a large pot one-third full with acorns, then cover with an equal volume of water. Bring to a boil, and boil until the water turns dark brown. Pour off the water and repeat the process several times. You may read that you should continue boiling in changes of water until the water remains clear, but that's bad advice. The water often remains dark long after any hint of bitterness is gone. Trust your taste buds instead of your eyes. Start tasting the acorns after the third or fourth change of water. When there's no trace of bitterness, your nuts are leached.

COLD LEACHING

There are a few methods for cold leaching acorns: using a toilet, using a jar, and using a colander with running water.

Toilet method. The easiest way to cold leach acorns is to use your toilet. To be clear: I'm talking about the toilet **tank**, *not* the toilet bowl. Empty the toilet tank, scrub it, then refill it with clean water.

Put your shelled acorns in a jelly bag and place the bag into the toilet tank. Each flush runs cold water through the nuts, leaching them of their bitterness. Taste test at intervals after 24 hours. You may need as long as 2 to 3 days, depending on how often you flush.

Jar method. If the idea of using the toilet makes you squirm, try the jar method. First you'll need to grind your shelled acorns. You can do this in a high-quality blender, like a Vitamix, or with a coffee bean grinder if you're doing a small batch.

Find a large, clear jar with a tight-fitting lid. Fill the jar halfway with ground acorn meal, then top it off with tap water. Close the lid, and give the jar a good shake, then move the jar to the refrigerator and let sit for 24 hours. The acorn meal will settle out of the water, and the water will turn brown as the tannins leach from the nuts. Carefully pour the water off the meal. Don't worry about getting every last drop. Refill the jar with water and replace the jar in the refrigerator. Let the jar sit for

24 hours, then pour off the water again. Repeat the process a third time, then taste the acorn meal. If it's bitter, continue to change the water every 24 hours until no trace of bitterness remains.

Running water method. If you're in a big hurry for cold leached acorn flour, try this method: Place a large colander in the sink and line it with a dish towel. Pour your shelled, ground acorns into the colander, then run a stream of cool water into the acorn meal and stir constantly for 8 minutes. You should be able to stir without spilling, which is why this is best done in small batches in a large colander. When done stirring, taste the slurry. If there is any bitter flavor, let the water run for another 2 or 3 minutes and taste again.

LONG-TERM STORAGE

For whole leached acorns, dry in a dehydrator on the lowest possible temperature. You must keep the temperature below 150°F (65°C) to avoid cooking the starch. If you don't have a dehydrator, you can dry your acorns in an oven or warming drawer, as long as the temperature is below 150°F (65°C). The nuts are fully dried when they are brittle and can be broken in half with a snap.

All acorns have a testa, which is a thin, bitter, papery skin located between the nut meat and the shell. The testas of white acorns adhere to the shells, but the testas of red acorns stick to the nuts. Hot leaching removes most testas, but if you cold leach, you'll need to rub off the testas before you cook with your acorns. Fortunately, after drying, the testas fall away with a gentle rubbing.

For leached acorn meal, once the bitterness has been leached via either the jar or the running water method, pour the meal out into the center of a dry towel. Gather the four corners of the towel together and twist the towel until water begins to drip from the bottom of the dish towel. Continue twisting and squeezing to remove as much water as you can. Warning: This will stain the dish towel, so don't use your finest family heirloom.

If you have a dehydrator with fruit leather sheets, spread the moist acorn meal across the sheets and set the temperature to the lowest possible setting. Depending on the humidity where you live, your meal will take between 12 and 24 hours to dry. Check it after several hours and break up any large clumps to speed the drying process. An oven or warming drawer will also work, as long as the temperature is below 150°F (65°C).

Once the acorns (whole or ground) have dried, they're ready to be measured, sealed, and stored. Acorns are high in fat, which may turn rancid if stored at room temperature, so freezing is recommended for long-term storage.

WHERE AND HOW TO FIND

- Trees require full sun to thrive.
- Plants grow almost everywhere, but not all oaks are created equal from the forager's point of view; look for trees that produce large nuts.
- Scrub oaks of the high desert produce few (if any!) teeny nuts.
- Look in parks, abandoned homesteads, and in residential neighborhoods (don't forage on private property without permission).

ID CHECKLIST

- Trees can be deciduous or evergreen depending on the species.
- Most oaks hold on to their dead leaves through the winter, which makes them stand out in the landscape—this is a helpful ID characteristic.
- Plants may be small and shrubby or single stemmed and more than 100 feet tall.
- Mature oaks are usually among the largest trees in the landscape.
- Trees may be wider than they are tall.
- Leaves are usually lobed, but some oaks do not have the characteristic lobes.
- Leaves are leathery, medium to dark green, and 2–10 inches long.
- Acorns have a point on the bottom and a cap on the top.
- The acorn cap may sit on just the top of the nut, or may cover almost the entire nut, depending on the species.
- No other nut looks like the acorn.

The rounded lobes of this oak leaf indicate that it's in the white oak family.

Sound, ripe acorns will separate from their caps when they have matured.

PERSIMMON

Diospyros virginiana

A.k.a.: winter plum, Jove's fruit, possumwood, simmon

Best part to eat: fruit

When to harvest: fall or winter, when the fruit is squishy (fully ripe)

I look forward to persimmon season every year. Ripe persimmon fruits are small, orange-brown balls of squishy, sweet deliciousness. How could you not be joyful with such tasty fruit?

There are two categories of persimmons: astringent and non-astringent. Non-astringent persimmons, like the Asian Fuyu, can be eaten when they're crisp, picked right off the tree. Astringent persimmons, like our native American persimmon, aren't ready to eat until they actually fall off the tree. They look and feel so soft and mushy you might think they're rotten. Oh, but they are not. Rumor has it persimmons can be harvested after the first frost, but don't be fooled. A tree full of persimmons is just a tease. If you want edible fruit, look *under* the tree.

I learned this the hard way. I'll never forget the shame I felt when I had to throw away that big bucket of unripe fruit. I tried everything to counterbalance the astringency but nothing worked. Since then I've read that nearly ripe persimmons can be ripened by putting them in a paper bag with either a banana or a ripe apple. Both of these fruits give off ethylene gas, which speeds the ripening process for the persimmons. But persimmons ripened this way will never have the rich flavor of a tree-ripened persimmon.

You might wonder how bad an unripe persimmon can be. Surely I must be exaggerating. No, I am not. The astringency is so severe that it makes the inside of your mouth feel dry and fuzzy. Your eyes will squint and you'll want to spit. On the other hand, a ripe persimmon is sublime; its pulp is silky and tastes of caramel.

HARVESTING

Persimmons don't all ripen at once. Fruit on different trees can ripen months apart, and fruit on the same tree may ripen over several weeks. If you find a heavily laden tree, keep checking it every few days so you can gather the fruit as it becomes ready.

It's perfectly all right to shake a branch to loosen ripe fruit. But taste any fruit you harvest this way to make sure it's fully ripe. Just one unripe persimmon can ruin a whole batch of fruit.

A perfectly ripe specimen will be custardy soft and the skin will be so thin it might break in your hand. When a super soft fruit hits the ground, it often splits wide open. Only persimmons that land on soft grass or other plants remain intact. This delicate and delicious fruit makes you work for your eating pleasure.

Persimmons fall from the tree when they are ripe.

FEASTING

Some people compare the flavor of our native persimmon to that of dates, and it's true they both have a natural sweetness and soft flesh. But that comparison does not do justice to the persimmon. Its fruit is superb when eaten fresh out of hand. Each fruit contains several good-size seeds, so spit them out if you're eating the fruit whole. If you're going to cook with the pulp, use a food mill to separate the seeds from the flesh. The processed pulp freezes well.

Steamed persimmon pudding is a classic American dessert. It's moist and sweet, and since this is a fruit that ripens in fall, it'll be available for your fall and winter holiday feasts. I also use persimmon pulp to make persimmon cookies and a frozen persimmon margarita that tastes as good as it looks. And it looks really, really good.

PERSIMMON
KNOW BEFORE YOU EAT

WHERE AND HOW TO FIND

- Wild trees are native to the eastern United States as far north as Connecticut and can also be found west of the Mississippi from Texas north to Nebraska.

- Plants grow best in full to part sun.

- Seeds are spread by skunks, opossums, deer, and raccoons.

ID CHECKLIST

- In the wild, persimmon trees may grow to be 15–20 feet tall; in rich, cultivated soils, they may grow to 80 feet.

- Whitish-green flowers are small (approximately ½ inch long) and tubular, with recurved petals once the bloom fully opens.

- Male and female flowers are usually borne on separate plants and look very similar, but you will only get fruit from female plants.

- Seeds are large and brown.

- Leaves are dark green, oval, and approximately 3–6 inches long.

- Leaves have a white midrib and are arranged alternately on the branch.

- Undersides of leaves are whitish-green and slightly fuzzy.

- Fall foliage is attractive and ranges from yellow to orange to red.

- Tree bark becomes darker and thicker with age and looks chunky, like alligator skin.

- Look for leafless trees bedecked with orange balls in fall.

- American persimmon fruit is 1–1½ inches in diameter.

- Each fruit has a pointy "beak" at the end of it.

unassuming persimmon flowers

persimmon foliage

alligator bark of the persimmon tree

If you have to pick the persimmon fruit off the tree, it isn't ready!

AMERICAN WILD PLUM

Prunus americana

A.k.a.: American plum, wild plum, red plum, August plum, hedge plum

Best part to eat: fruit

When to harvest: when ripe, usually late summer and fall

The American wild plum may grow as a tree (single stemmed) or shrub (multistemmed). In nature it often forms large thickets, as the plant spreads by underground roots as well as by seed. It is widely distributed across the United States and Canada and is often spread by birds or other animals dropping the pits after eating the fruit.

Wild plums are considerably smaller than cultivated plums, generally about 1 inch in diameter. Their skins are thicker than those of store-bought fruit. If you taste a wild plum and it's too tannic for your taste, try peeling it. Many of the tannins reside in the skin and using only the flesh may give you a more useful end product. But remember, most of the pectin is also in the skin, so if you're making jam or jelly (page 238), you might want to leave at least a few of the skins on. Or you can add commercial pectin to guarantee a good set.

Foragers disagree over whether to include wild plum skins in their cooking. I attribute this to the variability of wild plum fruit. The flavor varies widely from place to place and tree to tree, so taste a few plums before you harvest a passel. If you decide to leave the skins on, run them through a food processor after pitting them; they are definitely thicker and tougher than the skins of cultivated plums.

You can smell these wild plum flowers from a distance—so fragrant!

Ripe plums will come off the branch with the slightest touch; if you have to tug on the fruit, it isn't ready! Depending on where you forage, wild plums may be ripe from midsummer to midfall.

FEASTING

Wild plums are generally more tart than cultivated or store-bought plums. They contain natural pectin, which makes them great for jams and jellies, and they also make tasty barbecue sauces, ketchups, syrups (page 234), fruit leathers, and chutneys. The American plum is much more tannic than cultivated plums, which makes it an excellent fruit for wine (page 236), if you're a homebrewer.

If the only wild plums you find are too tannic for you to enjoy, try removing the skins before you cook with the flesh.

You can do this in several ways. Freeze and thaw the plums, or roast them in a 350°F (175°C) oven until the juices begin to flow. When the fruit is room temperature, you should be able to squeeze the flesh (and pits) out of the skins. You can also dip the fruit briefly in boiling water, then peel them, as you would do with tomatoes and peaches.

If you're fortunate enough to come across a perfectly delicious crop of wild plums, you might want to dry them between 125 and 135°F (50 and 55°C) to appreciate their pure, unadulterated flavor. Slice them in half, remove the pit, and dehydrate until they have a prune-like texture.

Fragrant wild plum flowers can be used to make a liqueur, and their flavor also infuses well in cream (page 240), for puddings and panna cottas.

Almond-Flavored Extract

You may have read that plum pits contain cyanide, which is almost true. They contain amygdalin, which becomes hydrogen cyanide when mixed with water. But that doesn't mean you can't enjoy the kernels inside the pits! With a little work you can use the kernels to make your own almond-flavored extract. You'll need to crack open each pit with a hammer to get at the kernel inside, then roast the kernels at 350°F (175°C) for 15 minutes to neutralize the amygdalin. Infuse the kernels in vodka or brandy (page 237) to make a delicious almond-flavored extract or infuse them in cream (page 240) for a fantastic ice cream.

OTHER SPECIES

While the wild American plum is the most widely distributed wild plum in the US and Canada, there are other tasty plums to look for when you're out foraging. Maybe you live near the ocean and find beach plums (*Prunus maritima*). Beach plums ripen to be dark purple and are native to the northeastern US.

Maybe the streets of your city are planted with cherry plums (*P. cerasifera*). These plum trees have purple foliage that is almost the exact same color as their ripe fruit. Or maybe you're lucky enough to find ruby red Chickasaw plums (*P. angustifolia*) where you forage. All of these are worth harvesting.

cherry plums

beach plums

Chickasaw plums

AMERICAN WILD PLUM
KNOW BEFORE YOU EAT

Wild plums look ripe before their flavor has fully developed. Taste one to be sure it's not too astringent, and if it is, wait another week, then try again.

WHERE AND HOW TO FIND

- Deciduous trees that grow best in full sun
- Drought tolerant but will also grow with average moisture
- Does not grow in waterlogged soil
- Seeds are often spread by birds and other animals, so look along fence lines, at the edges of fields, and in windbreaks or shelterbelts.

ID CHECKLIST

- Black knot fungus may encircle the branches of plum trees.

- Trees may grow to be 20–25 feet tall.

- Flowers emerge in early spring, before the foliage.

- Trees are easiest to spot in spring when they are covered with blooms.

- Flowers are strongly fragrant, with five white petals and many long, prominent stamens.

- Flowers are approximately 1 inch in diameter.

- Leaf shape is oval with pointed tips and toothed margins; foliage is arranged alternately on the branch.

- Leaves are 2½–4 inches long.

- Tree bark is marked by horizontal pores (lenticels) that allow for gas exchange and are typical of cherries and plums.

- Often thorny

- Ripe fruit may be pinkish-red or yellow.

- Ripe fruit should have a little bit of give to it when squeezed.

fragrant plum blossoms

lenticels

ROSE

Rosa species

A.k.a.: rose

Best part to eat: petals, hips

When to harvest: spring through fall (petals), hips (after first frost)

When I first started foraging for roses, I was only interested in the hips (the red/pink/orange fruits of roses). They're tasty, versatile, and full of vitamin C—during World War II, for example, the British gave women and children rose hip syrup as a vitamin supplement. But fragrant rose petals soon became another one of my favorite wild ingredients. Just note that if the petals have no fragrance, they will have no flavor, so stick your nose down into the flower before you harvest. And be sure to watch out for bees.

Most truly wild roses have pink flowers, although some are white. All wild roses have five petals and many are fragrant. It's only as roses have been hybridized for other features (more petals, disease resistance, and repeat blooming) that fragrance has fallen by the wayside as being less important. Clearly those rose hybridizers are not foragers. Wild roses of one kind or another grow in every state of the US. Two very common roses, multiflora rose (*Rosa multiflora*) and rugosa rose (*R. rugosa*), are considered feral in the US, having escaped cultivation, and they are wild and native to other parts of the planet, too.

R. multiflora is listed as a noxious weed in many states, and it is downright

Rugosa roses thrive in sandy soils and also tolerate salt spray. You'll often find them on beaches.

R. rugosa

R. multiflora

prohibited in others. It was introduced to the US in the late nineteenth century as a rootstock for ornamental roses, and the US Soil Conservation Service promoted it as a living fence and for erosion control. *R. multiflora* is a prolific plant and not particular about soil quality. It grows in both full sun and full shade, and often forms dense thickets with sharp, curved prickles that easily make holes in an unsuspecting T-shirt. Its flowers have a spicy fragrance and flavor. Feel free to harvest with impunity.

R. rugosa is sometimes called the beach plum because its fruit (the hips) is as large as some plums. This rose, although sometimes feral, is also often planted in sandy beach soils for its tolerance of salt and sand. The flowers are wonderfully fragrant (and tasty) and the hips are large, which makes them much more versatile and easy to work with than the mini hips of multiflora roses.

Any rose that hasn't been sprayed with toxic chemicals produces edible flowers and hips. Depending on where you live, rose hips ripen at the end of summer or the beginning of fall. They're persistent fruits, and linger on the plant until someone (or something) removes them. It's not unusual to see last year's shriveled hips still on the plant when new flowers bloom.

Some people harvest rose hips as soon as they ripen and others leave them on the plant to sweeten. Just ripe (or slightly underripe) rose hips will have more pectin (good for jelly), but will be less sweet.

FEASTING

Petals. Harvest rose petals while they are still fresh and dewy; they'll keep for a day or two in the refrigerator. Their flavor infuses well in cream (page 240), which can then be used to make ice cream or panna cotta, syrup (page 234), or baked goods. You can also make your own rose water.

Hips. Rose hips have a longer harvest season than rose petals. For the sweetest possible fruit, pick after a frost or two. It's less important what the rose hips look like and more important how they taste. The most delicious hips I ever harvested were on a feral rose in Denver in spring, after the hips had been on the plant all winter. They looked shriveled and dry, but the flavor was sweet and reminiscent of strawberries.

You'll need to process your rose hips before enjoying them. Inside each red fruit are many small seeds, surrounded by many small hairs, which are highly irritating to the throat. If you

These rose hips look wrinkled after a long winter but still have great flavor!

want to make jelly (page 238) or syrup (page 234), you can juice whole rose hips, no deseeding required. If you want to use rose hip pulp, you'll need to clean the seeds and hairs out of each hip, so look for large fruits like those produced by rugosa roses or dog roses (*R. canina*). Cut the fruit in half, scoop out the seeds and hairs, and discard them. Put the cleaned pulp in a pan and barely cover with water. Cook over low to medium heat until the water is absorbed and the pulp has softened. Run the pulp through a food mill. Then use it to make fruit leather, jam, and that Scandinavian classic—rose hip soup.

Rose hips store well in the freezer, or if you've got a dehydrator, you can dry the fruit at 95°F (35°C) and rehydrate it when you have time to play with your harvest. If you do the latter, save the water you use to rehydrate the hips ... it may come in handy in your recipe. When you have time to cook with your rose hips, stay away from copper or aluminum cookware. Copper can destroy the vitamin C in the hips, and aluminum dulls the bright red color of the fruit.

To use rose hip pulp, you'll need to scoop out the seeds and hairs first.

WHERE AND HOW TO FIND

- Wild and feral roses grow everywhere from sandy beaches to high deserts to shady woodlands.
- Some roses are well-behaved and others are rampantly aggressive.
- You may find cultivated roses at abandoned homesteads, in yards, and in parks.

ID CHECKLIST

- Wild roses look similar to cultivated roses but often have flatter flowers with fewer petals.
- Shrubs are perennial, deciduous, and woody.
- Stems are covered with prickles, not thorns (prickles are outgrowths of the epidermis of the plant stem, while thorns are modified branches or stems).
- Leaf margins are serrated.

- Leaves are 2–6 inches long and pinnate (small leaflets arranged along a central stem), usually with three to seven leaflets.
- While cultivated roses may have many petals, most wild roses have five petals, surrounded by five sepals, which form a green collar underneath the petals.
- Rose hips are the fruit of the rose and each one contains multiple seeds.
- Rose hips are generally orange to red.

flowers of the invasive multiflora rose

SUMAC

Rhus species

A.k.a.: skunkbush, basket bush

Best part to eat: fruit

When to harvest: when ripe; usually mid- to late summer

Before you ask about sumac being poisonous, let me explain. Yes, there is such a thing as poison sumac, but it's a pretty rare plant, growing primarily in wetlands east of the Mississippi. It's also *very* easy to differentiate between poison sumac and edible sumacs when the plants are in fruit. Poison sumac has loose, drooping clusters of white berries that emerge from between the leaves. Edible sumac has red fruit borne in terminal clusters (at the ends of branches). Since the only part of the plant I recommend eating is the fruit, the color makes it pretty easy to tell which is which.

There are many types of edible sumac in the United States, including smooth sumac (*Rhus glabra*), staghorn sumac (*R. typhina*), and three-leaved sumac (*R. trilobata*), among others. All produce red berries with varying degrees of sourness. While some people eat the young shoots of sumac stems, I'm not impressed enough by the flavor to go out of my way for them. I'm in it for the berries. The tart, red berries.

Sumac berries get their lemony flavor from a combination of acids that coat the fruit. These acids are washed away by rain, so gather your sumac as soon as possible after the berries ripen. Although the acids accumulate again after each rain, the berries become progressively less tart (and less tasty)

with each successive downpour. To test the tartness before you harvest, pop a single berry in your mouth. If it doesn't make you pucker up, just walk away.

Timing is key when it comes to harvesting sumac berries. Their color deepens before the flavor fully develops, so you can't rely on a visual to know when to harvest. Start tasting your sumac as soon as it's bright red, monitoring its developing tartness. Depending on where you forage, it should be ready from mid- to late summer.

The fruit of staghorn sumac is fuzzy.

Another reason not to wait too long to harvest is that large sumac cones (like those of smooth and staghorn sumac) are often colonized by caterpillars. Let's just say this makes them substantially less appetizing. Take a moment to imagine what the caterpillars are

three-leaved sumac (*R. trilobata*) fruit

doing in there, then tell me if you want to eat that.

Harvest your sumac fruit by cutting off whole cones where their stems join the branch. Cones can be dried by placing them in a paper bag and hanging them somewhere dark and dry for 2 to 4 weeks. Or break apart the cones and dry them at 95°F (35°C) in your dehydrator. Dried sumac should last for a year or two in an airtight jar.

FEASTING

If you've ever tasted za'atar, you've probably tasted sumac. The Middle Eastern species of sumac, tanner's sumac (*R. coriaria*), is a primary ingredient in this popular spice blend. You can easily make your own za'atar with local sumac and a few favorite herbs. Or you can use dried sumac alone to add a dash of tartness and color to breads, pasta, rice, fish, chicken, or pork.

Sumacade is a popular beverage among foragers, and most agree that cold brewing produces a tastier beverage. Boiling water can release bitter tannins in the sumac seeds, making the drink overly astringent. To make sumacade, add cold water to a jar with several sumac clusters and let it sit on the counter. When the color is bright red, taste the liquid. When it's tart enough to please you, strain off the solids and filter the liquid before serving. The hairs of some sumac fruits can be irritating to the throat.

You can run unsweetened sumacade through a SodaStream if you don't mind voiding your warranty (sugar will clog the machine). Or, if you have a soda siphon, you can carbonate sweetened sumacade, which makes a lovely cocktail mixer. Speaking of cocktails, try infusing gin, vodka, or rum with sumac fruit (page 237). You'll get exceptional color as well as flavor.

tanner's sumac (*R. coriaria*) fruit

SUMAC
KNOW BEFORE YOU EAT

WHERE AND HOW TO FIND

- Staghorn and smooth sumac often grow by the side of the road.

- All sumac is easy to spot when the fruit is ripe, even if you're going 50 miles per hour.

- Three-leaved sumac is often used in landscaping, as its form is more compact and bushier than staghorn or smooth sumac.

- All sumacs are sun-loving shrubs or small trees.

ID CHECKLIST

- Plants generally leaf out in mid-spring, after the crabapples bloom.

- Spread by underground rhizomes, plants often form thickets in nature.

- Trunks and branches of staghorn sumac are softly fuzzy, with a covering similar to the velvet of deer antlers.

- Staghorn and smooth sumac grow to be about 20 feet tall on average.

- Three-leaved sumac gets to be approximately 6–8 feet tall.

fuzzy staghorn sumac branch

staghorn sumac leaves and fruit

- Foliage of smooth and staghorn sumac is finely cut, with individual leaflets being long and narrow, with toothed margins; overall, leaves may be up to 2 feet long.

- Leaves of three-leaved sumacs are generally divided into three, fat lobes with toothed margins, and the foliage is 1–2 inches long.

- Leaves are arranged alternately on the branch.

- All sumacs have gorgeous fall foliage ranging from yellow to orange to deep red.

- Staghorn and smooth sumac cones can be 2–8 inches long.

- Staghorn berries are covered with fuzzy hairs; smooth sumac is smooth.

- Three-leaved sumac fruit is fuzzy and borne in small, roundish clusters approximately 1–1½ inches in diameter.

smooth sumac fruit

three-leaved sumac fruit

smooth sumac leaves

three-leaved sumac leaves

BANANA YUCCA

Yucca baccata

A.k.a.: Spanish bayonet, blue yucca, soapweed

Best part to eat: flowers, fruit

When to harvest: spring through summer (flowers), summer through fall (fruit)

Yuccas are succulent plants and all of them have edible parts. They should not be confused with yuca, which is another name for cassava. While yuca is edible, this is not about that.

Most people think of yuccas as denizens of the desert, and these plants are indeed drought tolerant and tough as nails. But they're also at home in containers and gardens in many different climates, and they're lovely to look at all year round, with their stiff foliage and persistent architecture.

Banana yucca is my favorite yucca. It's beautiful and delicious with curved, blue-green foliage that's edged with curled fibers. A mature plant may be 2 feet tall. Harsh winters may damage the leaves, but generally speaking these are evergreen plants.

All yuccas start life as basal rosettes of foliage. Their leaves are spiky, often described as swordlike, and as someone who has been pierced more than once by the astonishingly sharp tips of yucca foliage, I can tell you that these plants will draw blood.

Several friends report that eating raw flowers causes them to have an itchy throat, but neither my husband nor I experience that. You may hear that yucca pistils and stamens are bitter and/or toxic, and should be discarded. But bear in mind that yucca flowers are a traditional ingredient in many Central and South American cuisines, and there has been no report of yucca blossom–related mass fatalities south of our border. I feel perfectly confident eating them.

While all yuccas have edible flowers, banana yucca is particularly generous. It produces large, sweet fruits (hence its common name) in addition to its flavorful blooms. However, because producing a fruit crop takes a lot of energy from the plant, banana yucca will not fruit every year. Depending on your location, fruit ripens in early to midfall. The fruit remains green even when ripe; give it a gentle squeeze and if you feel a little give, the fruit is ready to harvest.

FEASTING

Flowers. There are lots of recipes for yucca blossoms in eggs, soups, and stews. But the first time you try the flowers, prepare them simply so you can get acquainted with their flavor. People describe it as resembling that of artichoke, but I don't agree. I find it milder than that. You may detect a tiny bit of bitterness, depending on how sensitive you are to bitter flavors. Remember, bitter doesn't mean bad. Arugula and radicchio are bitter greens that you pay good money for at the supermarket. Wash your yucca blossoms well when

Flower Stalks?

Some foragers mention that immature yucca flower stalks are edible if harvested while young and tender. I'm sure this is true, but since I value the flowers and fruit of this plant, I'm not willing to sacrifice either in order to eat the bloom stalk as a green shoot. We all make our choices in life and that's mine.

you get them home. Ants and other insects are quite fond of the flowers. Fortunately, they're easy to spot against the pale white blooms.

Fruits. Banana yucca produces tasty fruit, but they come with a caveat. The pollinators of yucca flowers are highly specialized yucca moths. The female yucca moth makes a hole in the base of an unpollinated flower and lays her eggs in the flower's ovary. After laying her eggs, she pollinates the flower, thus providing food for the developing larvae. They live inside the maturing fruit and eat the seeds, eventually burrowing out and down into the ground to make their cocoons. Bring home a bunch of ripe fruit and you may well be bringing home the resident larvae within. If you're not interested in the additional protein, put the fruit in the freezer for a few days. The larvae will exit the fruit and die, leaving you the yucca fruit to enjoy.

Yucca fruit has *loads* of seeds inside. Roast the fruit (400°F [200°C] for 30 minutes), then slice them in half, remove the seeds, and scoop out the naturally sweet flesh.

WHERE AND HOW TO FIND

- Grows best in full sun and in dry or well-drained soils
- Often found in large quantities in neglected spaces
- Look for yuccas in early to midsummer (depending on where you forage).
- Easiest to spot when their flower spikes are in bloom

ID CHECKLIST

- Blue-green rosette of spiky foliage
- Central bloom stalk appearing in late spring, usually taller than the foliage
- White, downward-hanging, bell-shaped flowers, often flushed with pink
- Pollinated flowers sometimes followed by large, green, oval fruit, maturing to 6 inches long
- Wide-leaved yuccas produce edible fruit.
- Narrow-leaved yucca species produce fruit, but it's generally too fibrous to be tasty.

swordlike foliage

flowers at the perfect stage for harvesting

This fruit is ripe and ready to harvest.

CHAPTER 4

Edibles from
DAPPLED EDGES & SHADY PLACES

These plants appreciate a little shade.
Look for them at the edges of woods,
in neighborhood parks, and
along country roads.

BURDOCK

Arctium lappa, A. minus

A.k.a.: beggar's buttons, gobo, greater burdock, lesser burdock

Best part to eat: flower stems, roots

When to harvest: before flowering (flower stems), spring/fall (roots)

You've probably walked past burdock multiple times, wondering, "What is that giant plant?!" It's a common roadside weed of impressive proportions: Leaves can be 2 feet long, flower stalks may be 5 feet tall, and the roots can be 3 feet long. It's not bad looking, it's a well-known medicinal plant, and several parts are edible, yet we still consider it a weed. Go figure.

In Japan, burdock root is sold as the vegetable *gobo* and served pickled, or slivered and sautéed in tamari sauce. When grown as a commercial crop, burdock is planted in sand, which makes digging it up much less challenging than harvesting it from the wild. In rocky, hard soil burdock root takes hold and won't let go. Harvesting wild burdock root isn't like pulling up a bunch of potatoes. It takes serious digging.

Burdock flower stalks are a much easier harvest. They have a flavor reminiscent of artichokes, and in my opinion taste even better than burdock root. If you come across a big patch of burdock at the right stage of development, it's easy to gather a substantial number of flower stalks in a short time.

Flowers are followed by fruits with hooks on them, which cling to animal fur and human clothing. These were the inspiration for Velcro.

Burdock flowers superficially resemble thistle flowers.

Burdock leaves are not delicious but are distinctive looking, making the plant easy to identify.

Note the woman's size 8 shoe for scale.

HARVESTING

Burdock is a biennial plant. First-year growth is entirely vegetative (roots, shoots, and leaves). If you're after the burdock root, harvest it in fall of the first year or early spring of the second year, when the roots are plump and full of nutrition. At the beginning of the second year, the burdock plant uses that stored energy to produce its flower stalk. And lest you feel sad about robbing the burdock plant of its flower stalk (because, yes, I'm going to suggest you harvest the root), please don't. Burdock is listed as an invasive species in several states; you will not make a dent in the population.

If you're after the burdock flower stalk, harvest in late spring or early summer of the second year. Keep an eye on the plant and watch for the flower stalk forming at the center. You'll want to harvest before it blooms; usually it will be 2 to 3 feet tall at this time. Cut off the flower stem as close to the ground as possible, and remove the leaves. The flower stem will be anywhere from 1/2 to 1 1/2 inches thick.

Turn the stem upside down. If you notice a hollow at the center of the stem, that bottom portion is too tough to be delicious. In which case, trim the stem from the bottom up, a few inches at a time, until you reach solid stem. Next, you'll need to peel it. Looking at the bottom of the stem, it's easy to see the difference between the bitter, fibrous outer covering and the tender, pale interior (that is, the tasty part). Use a sharp paring knife to peel off the outer skin.

FEASTING

While some foragers insist the young leaves of burdock are edible, I have never found them tasty. I focus on the roots and immature flower stalks. That's where the deliciousness lies.

Roots. In Japan, burdock root is often served as kinpira: peeled, sliced into matchsticks, and braised in mirin, sake, and soy sauce. If roots are harvested at the end of their first season, they may be tender enough that no peeling is necessary. If so, just give them a good scrub. In spring of their second year, you may want to peel them. After washing the root, take a bite of the raw root and decide if the skin is too fibrous to be pleasant. A simple roast (sliced into coins, tossed in olive oil, salt, and

pepper, and baked for 15 to 20 minutes at 400°F [200°C]) makes a delicious side dish and showcases burdock's nutty, earthy flavor. The root can also be used in mashes, stir-fries, and gratins.

Flower stalks. Burdock flower stalks can be served as a side dish or added to pasta, casseroles, or salads. Try chopping the peeled stalk into rough chunks, boiling until it's easily pierced with a fork (this takes longer than you might expect: 20 to 30 minutes), then serving with butter, salt, and pepper.

Yes, it's true. Burdock seed heads inspired the invention of Velcro with their grabby hooks.

WHERE AND HOW TO FIND

- Grows in full sun and part shade
- Often colonizes in disturbed soils, such as roadsides, empty lots, and the edges of fields
- Highly adaptable; prefers rich, moist soils but will tolerate a wide range of growing conditions

You'll want to peel the woody bark off second-year burdock roots.

ID CHECKLIST

- Biennial plant
- First-year growth produces a basal rosette of foliage.
- Leaves are medium green, have a rough surface and wavy edges, and are oval or heart-shaped.
- Leaves are large (up to 2 feet long for both species) with prominent white or red veins; they are sometimes confused with rhubarb leaves.
- Undersides of leaves are whitish-green and hairy.
- Lower leaves of greater burdock (*Arctium lappa*) have solid leafstalks and are grooved; lower leaves of lesser burdock (*A. minus*) usually have hollow leafstalks and are grooved.
- Second-year leaves are arranged alternately on the flower stalk and are smaller than basal foliage.
- Flowers appear in midsummer.
- Flower stalks of greater burdock may grow to be 8 feet tall; flower stalks of lesser burdock usually top off at about 5 feet tall.
- Flowers resemble thistle flowers, with bristly pink to purple florets.
- Flowers of greater burdock are 1–1½ inches in diameter; flowers of lesser burdock are about ½–1 inch in diameter.
- Fruits have hooks and will cling to clothing and animal fur.

NORTHERN BAYBERRY

Morella pensylvanica

A.k.a.: Pennsylvania bay, bayberry, candleberry, waxberry, *Myrica pensylvanica*

Best part to eat: leaves

When to harvest: any time

Do you like cooking with bay leaf but live somewhere too cold to forage for it or grow it yourself? If so, let me introduce you to northern bayberry. It is a tough, cold-hardy plant with leaves that have a very similar flavor to that of traditional bay leaf. Northern bayberry is native to the northeastern United States and Canada, tolerates salt spray well, and is often found growing in long swaths along country roads. It's an attractive shrub that will do well in any part of the country. You might consider planting one yourself. I did!

The gray-blue fruits of northern bayberry are pretty (though inedible), and attract birds to the garden. The plant is dioecious, which means male and female flowers grow on separate plants. If you're in it for the waxy berries, you'll need both a male plant (to pollinate) and a female plant (to bear fruit). If you're interested in the flavor of the leaves, you don't need to worry about the sex of the shrubs you find. Male and female shrubs produce equally flavorful foliage.

As a side note, the waxy component of northern bayberry fruit has been a traditional ingredient in candle and soap making since colonial times. It's a process that involves repeated boilings and skimmings of the ripe fruit. The candles may be brittle, but the scent is lovely and not overwhelming.

The waxy covering of northern bayberry fruit was used to make candles in colonial New England.

FEASTING

Drying intensifies the flavor of northern bayberry leaves, so harvest them fresh, then dry them for year-round use. You can either dry individual leaves in a dehydrator at 95°F (35°C), or bundle the stems together with an elastic band and hang them somewhere dry and out of direct sun. When drying is complete, store the dried bayberry leaves in a glass jar with a tight-fitting lid.

If you're a fan of herbal spirits, try infusing vodka or gin with northern bayberry leaves (page 237). They lend a subtle but excellent flavor.

You can use northern bayberry leaves in any recipe that calls for bay leaf (*Laurus nobilis*), but the flavor of northern bayberry is less strong, so use twice as many leaves. Just remember to remove the leaves before serving.

WHERE AND HOW TO FIND

- Grows best in full to part sun
- Woody, deciduous shrub that loses its leaves in winter and leafs out again in spring
- Tolerates a range of soils as well as poor soil nutrition
- Often forms large colonies

ID CHECKLIST

- Shrubs may grow to be 6–8 feet tall but are often shorter, depending on growing conditions.
- Oblong leaves are arranged alternately on the stem.
- Leaves are 2–4 inches long and 1½ inches wide with a pronounced, whitish middle vein.
- Leaves are medium to dark green, glossy, and somewhat leathery.
- Leaf margins are slightly wavy.
- Plants branch freely; lower stems may be bare, but foliage is densely clustered at the top of each branch.
- Leaves and stems smell like culinary bay leaves when crushed (an important identification characteristic).
- Small flowers are not visually impressive, with the female flowers being smaller than the male flowers.
- Fruit grows in clusters along the stems and stands out due to its waxy, gray-white coating.

Northern bayberry often forms large thickets.

POKEWEED
Phytolacca americana

A.k.a.: poke sallet, poke, polk, inkberry, American pokeberry

Best part to eat: young leaves and stems

When to harvest: when stems are tender and before flowering

Immortalized in Elvis Presley's version of "Polk Salad Annie" (please Google it, it's great), this edible green has been a traditional food (especially in the southeastern United States) for many years. In fact, until the year 2000 you could buy canned poke sallet greens, but as demand for commercially produced greens decreased, so did profitability and availability. Now, if you want to experience their flavor, you'll have to forage for them yourself.

Only the young leaves and stems of pokeweed are edible. The berries have been used for ink and dyes, and the root has a history as a medicinal herb, but neither berries nor root should be consumed as food.

HARVESTING

Pokeweed should be harvested before it begins to flower, while the tips of the stems are tender and easy to snap off with your hand. This young, most tender part of the plant is less fibrous than the rest of the plant and is known as the meristematic growth. This tissue growth occurs in parts of a plant (concentrated in the tips of the roots and shoots) where cell division rapidly takes place. If you find pokeweed that's waist high but you can easily snap off the last 6 to 8 inches and the plant has not yet started to bloom, it's safe to eat.

FEASTING

Pokeweed should never be eaten raw; consumption of raw pokeweed can lead to severe gastrointestinal distress. Boil leaves for 10 minutes, then drain. Take a small bite. If there's any bitterness, add fresh water and boil again for 5 minutes. Taste again. You probably won't need more than two boils, but if the pokeweed still tastes bitter, boil it again for 5 minutes.

Traditional poke sallet is made by boiling the terminal leaves, then frying them in bacon fat with onions and bacon (or shreds of meat from a ham hock) and dousing them with a little apple cider vinegar. It's delicious. You can prepare the tender young stems of pokeweed in the same way, but because they take longer to cook (they're thicker than the leaves), you'll want to boil them separately from the greens, then combine them in the frying pan with the bacon fat. Pokeweed stems are also tasty when boiled, rolled in cornmeal, and fried.

If you'd like to preserve your pokeweed for future use, boil it once, then freeze. Vacuum sealing before freezing helps eliminate freezer burn.

Myths about Toxicity

Some people think pokeweed is a poisonous plant. This simply isn't true. The berries and roots should not be eaten, but the young leaves and stems are perfectly edible, if harvested and prepared properly. Many of our everyday food plants are toxic if you eat the wrong part or prepare it in the wrong way. Raw potatoes contain solanine, which can cause nausea and diarrhea. Raw kidney beans can have similarly unpleasant effects. But nobody goes around telling you potatoes and kidney beans are poisonous, do they?

Other myths about pokeweed center on when it's safe to harvest. Some people say to harvest the young stems only when they are 6 inches long; others say you shouldn't harvest pokeweed once the stems have started to branch or show any red color, or that you need to boil pokeweed in three changes of water. None of these things are true. The only guidelines you need to remember are as follows: Harvest the meristematic stems and leaves before the plant flowers, and boil in fresh water until all bitterness is gone.

POKEWEED
KNOW BEFORE YOU EAT

WHERE AND HOW TO FIND

- One of the earliest greens to emerge in spring
- Start looking when the daffodils bloom.
- Likes disturbed soils; look in sunny fields, neglected spaces, and along the edges of woodlands.
- Easy to spot in late summer and early fall when it's tall and full of dark purple berries, but don't harvest then
- The previous year's tall (4–8 feet), light tan-colored stems often remain standing through winter.
- New shoots emerge from the base of last year's growth.
- Perennial plant that returns year after year
- Widely distributed across the US except for the northern Midwest, Rockies, and driest American deserts
- Harvest young leaves and stems in early spring.

ID CHECKLIST

- Herbaceous perennial growing to 4–8 feet tall at maturity
- Leaves are arranged alternately on the stem of the plant.
- Leaves have smooth edges.
- Leaf veins have a definite pattern.
- Stems are smooth and round.
- Stems branch freely after about 18 inches.

Both the leaves and the tender stems of pokeweed are edible.

The flower tells you this pokeweed is no longer at the right stage for harvesting.

- In sunny locations, the stems of pokeweed turn red.
- Small white flowers are held in narrow clusters at the ends of branches, starting in early summer; clusters may be either upright or drooping.
- Flowers are followed by green fruits that ripen to dark purple, juicy berries.

STINGING NETTLE

Urtica dioica

A.k.a.: common nettle, burn nettle

Best part to eat: leaves

When to harvest: before flowering (generally in spring)

Before I ever saw a stinging nettle, I felt its sting. I was walking through a field with sandals on and felt a sharp sting on the top of my foot. I thought it might be a yellow jacket or a red ant, but when I looked down, I saw a small, unremarkable plant, with stems covered in innocent-looking hairs. Ha. Little did I know that those tiny, hollow hairs on the stems and undersides of the leaves contain chemicals, including formic acid and histamine. When these hairs are broken, they release their chemicals, causing the infamous sting.

My foot swelled up for a few hours; the redness and itching lasted longer. Some foragers pick nettles barehanded, but I don't. If I run across a surprise nettle patch, I protect my hand with whatever I've got: a bandana, a baggie, a sock. I'm not going home without those nettles!

Stinging nettle is a perennial plant that reproduces both by underground rhizomes and by seed. Nettles are most common in moist soils and full sun but will also grow in dappled light. They can grow to be 2 to 6 feet tall, and their leaves are elliptical and roughly toothed, with pointed tips. Nettle flowers are small and green-brown, dangling in short chains from the leaf axils. The leaves roughly resemble mint leaves, but they have no smell and you definitely wouldn't want to chew on a raw nettle leaf!

Beware the hairs!

HARVESTING

Nettles are most tasty and tender in spring, before they bloom. Use leather gloves (the stinging hairs easily penetrate soft cloth) to pinch off the top several pairs of leaves and stem. By the time the plant blooms, it's usually tough and fibrous. You may hear rumors that mature nettles contribute to the formation of kidney stones or irritate the urinary tract. I've looked for peer-reviewed science to support this, but haven't found any. However, since young nettles are tasty nettles, I have no problem sticking with the pre-flowering plants.

The small flowers on this nettle indicate it's too old to be delicious.

When you find a good nettle patch, visit early and often. By harvesting every 1 to 2 weeks, you can prolong the tasty season. Snipping off the top 6 to 8 inches of the plant prevents it from producing flowers and lets you harvest for months instead of weeks.

Pro tip: If you get stung by nettles, look around for dock (page 34). Mash up a few of the young leaves from the center of the dock plant to release the mucilage, then apply this to your sting. The swelling won't go down, but the mashed dock should relieve some of the pain.

FEASTING

Nettle stingers are destroyed by cooking and drying. Some people dry the leaves, then grind them to make a powder, which they use for tea or as a soup base. I think more flavor is preserved by blanching the nettles, which can then be frozen and stored for up to a year. Plus, that way you get the potlikker (the water the nettles were blanched in), which can be drunk as tea or used in a cocktail. That's right. You heard me. A nettle cocktail.

Stinging nettles reduce in volume when cooked, the same way spinach does. People compare the flavor of nettles to that of spinach, but I think it's darker and richer than spinach. You can use cooked nettles in just about any way you'd use spinach: frittatas, quiches, stir-fries, soups, or pitas.

While some foragers claim to eat raw nettle leaves, I'm pretty sure it involves some intricate leaf origami. Having been stung on the foot, arms, legs, and hands, I'm unwilling to risk the possible pain of being stung *inside my mouth*! If you must eat your nettles raw, run them through a juicer or use a blender to get a highly nutritious and brilliantly colored green juice.

Many nutritionists consider nettles to be a superfood. They're rich in vitamins A and C, as well as calcium, iron, manganese, and potassium. But I don't care about any of that. I love nettles because they taste good.

WHERE AND HOW TO FIND

- Perennial plants that are usually found in sunny, moist spots

- Emerges in early spring

- Spread by rhizomes and by seed, and will often form thick clumps

ID CHECKLIST

- Leaves are usually 2–5 inches long and arranged in opposite pairs on the stem.

- Leaves are widest near the base (lanceolate) with pointed tips, serrated margins, and a strong, impressed pattern of veins.

- Stem is square and hollow.

- Leaves and stems are covered with stinging hairs called trichomes.

- Tassles of small green-brown flowers emerge from leaf axils.

- Mature height is 2–6 feet.

Note the characteristic quilted pattern of the leaves.

These hairs look innocuous, but don't be fooled! They sting.

WOOD NETTLE

Laportea canadensis

A.k.a.: Canada nettle

Best part to eat: leaves and young stems

When to harvest: before flowering (spring through early summer)

Should you find yourself thinking wood nettles are the poor cousin of stinging nettles, think again! Most foragers consider wood nettles to be more flavorful than stinging nettles. What's more, the young stems of wood nettles are a choice edible, while the stems of stinging nettles are not.

Young wood nettles look a lot like stinging nettles, but as they mature, the leaves become noticeably wider and longer than those of stinging nettles. Also, stinging nettles have opposite leaves, while wood nettle foliage is arranged alternately on the stem. And as the name indicates, wood nettles grow in the woods, usually in part to full shade. Stinging nettles grow best in full sun.

Wood nettles pop up later than stinging nettles, which expands your usable nettle harvest season. "Stinging" may not be part of their name, but wood nettles actually have more, larger stingers than stinging nettles, so even if you're one of those brave souls who picks stinging nettles with bare hands, you'll probably want to use gloves to harvest wood nettles. Why suffer needlessly?

Don't let the prickliness discourage you. Wood nettles are delicious, and you'll get more usable harvest from each plant than you would with stinging nettles. Not only are the stems quite tasty but the leaves are larger as well.

wood nettle

stinging nettle

FEASTING

When wood nettles first emerge in spring, they are mostly stem with just a few leaves clustered at the top. Young growth has fewer stinging hairs, but I'd still use gloves to harvest. At this stage, blanching the stems and leaves gives you a delicious vegetable that can honestly be compared to asparagus. (It bugs me how any shoot vegetable is automatically compared to asparagus, but in this case it's accurate.)

More mature wood nettle leaves taste even more like spinach than stinging nettles, and you can use the foliage any way you'd use spinach. When the leaves have expanded, harvest the top 4 to 6 inches (usually the last two pairs of leaves). Like spinach, wood nettles reduce in volume quite a bit in cooking.

To disarm the stingers, blanch or steam your wood nettles for at least 30 seconds, then freeze them to preserve. You may also can your wood nettles, but both flavor and texture are better preserved by freezing. Wood nettles dehydrated at 95°F (35°C) can be used to make tea, or can be ground into a powder and added to soups and stews for a nutritional boost, although they retain very little flavor when dried.

WOOD NETTLE
KNOW BEFORE YOU EAT

WHERE AND HOW TO FIND

- Grows primarily in woods with rich, moist soil, often along streams
- Perennial plant that will return to the same spot year after year
- Spread by both rhizomes and seeds, and will often form large colonies

ID CHECKLIST

- Foliage is oval with pointy tips and a deeply impressed pattern of veins.
- Leaves are medium green, up to 6 inches long and 4 inches wide.
- Leaves are borne on long leaf stems (leafstalks are also known as petioles).
- Leaf margins are serrated.
- Leaves are arranged alternately on the stem, although new leaves appear opposite when they first emerge.
- Central stem has a zigzag appearance.
- Leaves, petioles, and stems are covered with stinging hairs.
- Flowers are borne in small clusters (male flowers) from leaf axils and larger, showier (female) terminal clusters.
- Mature plants may grow to be 5 feet tall.

Stinging nettle flowers are small and unassuming.

The female flowers of wood nettle are showy and quite pretty.

CHAPTER 5

Plants That Like
WET
FEET

Some of these plants grow in
standing water, some in tidal marshes,
and some in soggy or moist soils.
One place you *won't* find them is in
dry soils . . . these are moisture lovers!

CATTAIL

Typha latifolia, T. angustifolia

A.k.a.: punks, bulrush, Cossack asparagus

Best part to eat: young shoots, male flowers

When to harvest: early spring (young shoots), late spring (male flowers)

Cattails spread by underground rhizomes and by seed. You'll often find them growing in large clumps, either in water (ponds, lakes, and rivers) or wet ground (drainage ditches or seasonal streambeds). They grow best in full sun. Cattails should be harvested from clean water only.

The two most common cattail species in the United States are common cattail (*Typha latifolia*) and narrow-leaf cattail (*T. angustifolia*). These two species hybridize naturally, making it difficult to differentiate them. Fortunately, you don't have to! They can be used in the same ways.

HARVESTING

To harvest young cattail shoots, cut off the stem as close to the base of the plant as possible. (Yes, you'll probably have to get wet!) Peel away the outer leaves to reveal the tender white heart of the plant, and cut off the tough, green, upper part of the shoot. Your hands will end up covered in a mucilaginous substance.

Male and female flowers are enclosed in a green sheath at the top of a tall, narrow, round flower stem. The flower stalk may be 3 to 6 inches long, with male flowers at the top of the stalk, and female flowers underneath. There is a clear dividing line between the male and female sections of the stalk. You won't be able to spot the sheathed flowers until you get up close and can see the difference between the rounded flower stems and the flat leaves. Harvest the flowers when they are still sheathed; cut off the male portion of the flower, just above the dividing line on the flower spike. If the male flowers have started to open, they will show bright yellow pollen. You want to harvest the flowers before that happens.

FEASTING

Euell Gibbons, the famous twentieth-century American forager, called cattails "the supermarket of the swamp." He got that right. Cattails have multiple edible parts, some more worthy of admiration than others.

Shoots. Tender young shoots of cattails have a mild cucumber flavor and are wonderful raw or cooked in stir-fries. Remember to peel them as described in the harvesting section.

Flowers. Cattail flowers are also edible, although I find only the male flowers worth harvesting. Female flowers taste fine, but offer very little substance. The immature male flowers of cattails are something I look forward to every year. They have a barely sweet, cornlike flavor, and are wonderful in breakfast tacos and egg dishes.

Rinse and steam the flowers for about 10 minutes. Once they're cool enough to handle, use a fork to scrape the male flowers off the thin midrib to which they cling.

Roots. Mature roots, called rhizomes, are starchy but have a tough core; you'll need to pound them to release the starch. Do this in late fall or early spring, when the rhizomes are full of stored nutrition. (Honestly, unless you're in a survival situation, I wouldn't bother with this. There's no deliciousness, only sustenance.) Immature rhizomes, harvested in late summer, are more tender, and they can be steamed or boiled. This is more a novelty than a meal.

Pollen. Cattail pollen is cool to collect, but be sure to sift it multiple times to get rid of the many insects that feed on the protein-rich pollen. Cattail pollen can be substituted for one-quarter to one-half of the traditional flour in a recipe. It adds nice color to pancakes, crackers, and flatbreads.

This pollen is ripe for harvesting.

Yellow flag iris is not edible! Learn to tell the difference.

POISONOUS LOOK-ALIKE

If you scout your cattails when they're in the "cigar flower" stage, you won't confuse them for anything else. Early in the growing season, you should be able to see last year's dried brown stems (with their attached cigars!), which will help you avoid confusion.

Yellow flag iris (*Iris pseudacorus*) may grow alongside cattails, but it is not edible. In bloom, yellow flag iris is easy to differentiate from cattails, with its yellow flower. Like cattail leaves, yellow flag iris leaves are also flat, but they have a distinctive midrib, which cattails do not have. Also, cattails are oval at the base and irises are flat at the base.

WHERE AND HOW TO FIND

- Mostly grows in standing water; you can also find it in soggy soil
- Perennial plant that spreads by rhizomes (edible rhizomes!) and often forms thickets over time
- Most abundant in full sun

ID CHECKLIST

- Plants are most easily identified when they're at their "cigar on a stick" stage, but don't eat them then; go back in spring and early summer.
- Foliage is flat, sword-shaped, and blue-green or gray-green with overlapping leaf bases.
- Base of the plant, where leaves come together, is oval (an important identification characteristic).
- Leaves may grow to be 8–9 feet tall.
- Flowers are borne on a smooth, round stem.
- Immature flowers are enclosed in green sheaths, making them difficult to spot from far away.
- Immature flowers are green and form a cylinder around the flower stem.
- Male flowers (top) and female flowers (bottom) are separated by a line of demarcation.
- Male flowers ripen to expose yellow pollen.
- Male flowers die back after pollen is dispersed.
- Female flowers ripen to form the familiar brown cigar, often persisting through winter.

oval leaf bases

Note the round flower stalk just to the left of the central, flat leaf.

CRANBERRY

Vaccinium macrocarpon, V. oxycoccos

A.k.a.: bearberry, fenberry, mossberry

Best part to eat: fruit

When to harvest: when ripe, usually fall

That's right, folks, the very same fruit you buy in bags from the grocery store every Thanksgiving can be yours for the taking. And you don't need to have a nearby bog to forage for wild cranberries!

Several species of wild cranberries can be found across the Northern Hemisphere, but large cranberry (*Vaccinium macrocarpon*) and small cranberry (*V. oxycoccos*) are the two most common. Both are short, trailing perennial shrubs or vines (botanists do not agree on this; foragers don't need to worry about it) that produce small white or pink flowers followed by tart red fruit.

Large cranberry produces slightly larger fruit (go figure!) and usually grows in wetter soils. Its leaves have blunt tips and are flat. The fruit of small cranberry may be rounder than the more oval large cranberries. The foliage of small cranberry has pointed tips and its margins are slightly rolled under. Although neither type is a large plant, small cranberry is smaller than large cranberry.

Commercial cranberries are grown in constructed bogs. In nature, you'll find them growing with damp feet but not swimming. Even commercial cranberries don't grow in water most of the year. The bogs are flooded as harvest time nears to make the harvest easier. Think about it: Floating berries are easier to gather than fruit growing on 8-inch tall shrubs. Alas, if you're foraging for cranberries, you're going to have to bend over. The good news is that "dry-picked" cranberries are less likely to be bruised and will last longer than "wet-picked."

Cranberries are persistent fruit, and while they ripen in late September to November, they'll stay on the plant through winter, depending on where you forage and how many hungry animals live nearby. Some people say the fruit is ruined by frost, but I promise you that is not true. After a few frosts, the fruit may be slightly wrinkled, but the flavor is still there.

When you find a cranberry patch, don't be discouraged if at first you don't see much fruit. Get down low to the ground and push aside the foliage. Many cranberries are borne low on the plants and may not be visible at first glance.

FEASTING

Freshly harvested cranberries will keep in the fridge for several weeks. They also freeze well, so if you don't have time to work with them immediately after harvest, rinse, dry, and vacuum seal your fruit before freezing.

Since wild cranberries are genetically the same as store-bought cranberries, you can use them the same way. Fresh cranberries can be combined with crabapples and rose hips to make a fantastic, jewel-toned chutney. They also make a great fruit tart and a fruity infused gin (page 237). And because they are so naturally high in pectin, you can combine them with low-pectin fruits to create interesting, sweet-tart jams and jellies (page 238).

CRANBERRY
KNOW BEFORE YOU EAT

Note the pointed leaf tips of small cranberry.

WHERE AND HOW TO FIND

- Grows on the banks of lakes and ponds as well as in bogs and in damp, acidic soils
- Often grows with blueberries, white pines, sweet fern, sphagnum moss, and other acid-loving plants
- Only native to the Northern Hemisphere
- Grows best in full sun

ID CHECKLIST

- Small, evergreen shrubs average 8–12 inches high.
- Stems are slim and woody.
- Evergreen leaves are medium to dark green, small, and leathery.
- Foliage is oval and about ½–1 inch long.
- Undersides of leaves are paler green than tops of leaves.
- Leaves of small cranberry have pointed tips and recurved leaf margins, while the tips of large cranberry are blunt and leaves are flat.
- Foliage is arranged alternately on the stem.
- White or pink flowers are less than ½ inch long with four reflexed petals.
- Flowers bloom in early to midsummer.
- Fruit is borne on very thin stems and may be (but isn't always) larger than foliage.
- Immature fruit is green and ripens to pink, then red.
- In fall, leaves take on a red color.

Cranberry flowers may be white or pink. They all have four reflexed petals.

ripe cranberry fruit

large cranberry

JAPANESE KNOTWEED

Reynoutria japonica

A.k.a.: Asian knotweed, fleece flower, donkey rhubarb, pea shooters

Best part to eat: young stems

When to harvest: spring

Japanese knotweed is a prolific and aggressive weed, and most homeowners hate it. Not me. I celebrate a good patch of this delicious plant, as long as it's not encroaching on my garden or the foundation of my home.

Generally, Japanese knotweed prefers damp soils. It grows in sun or shade, in roadside ditches, on river banks, in backyards, and in city parks. In other words, it's hard to find someplace Japanese knotweed *doesn't* grow. And while it prefers damp soils, it will grow in soils with average moisture.

Japanese knotweed spreads by underground stolons (runners), and it also produces thousands of seeds per plant. In Darwinian terms, it's a very successful plant. Originally introduced to the United States as an ornamental plant in the late 1800s, it was also used to create windbreaks and to stabilize erosion. Oops! Turns out Japanese knotweed not only crowds out some native plants but can also threaten hardscapes (like cement foundations) with its muscular root system. It's now illegal to plant Japanese knotweed anywhere in the UK, and parts of the US are following suit.

As Japanese knotweed matures it gets tough and fibrous, and so it requires peeling. Since I'm a lazy forager, I harvest young, tender stalks that don't require peeling. You may have read that only the very short, young stalks of Japanese knotweed are suitable for eating, but this isn't true. If you can easily snap off the top of the stem (with a satisfying pop), you're good to go. If it's too tough to snap by hand,

A Note on Names

Japanese knotweed has been assigned to several different genera over the years. You may see it called *Reynoutria, Fallopia,* or *Polygonum.*

check further up the stem for a spot tender enough to break. By midsummer in most places, the entirety of the stem will be too tough to harvest.

I look forward to the Japanese knotweed harvest every spring, knowing how easy it is to preserve large quantities of it, and understanding that it's okay to be greedy with this plant. Japanese knotweed is one plant you probably couldn't eradicate if you tried.

FEASTING

Stems may be as thick as your thumb or as slim as a pencil. As long as they're flexible, they're good to eat. Remove all but the last pair of leaves before cooking. Some people compare the flavor of Japanese knotweed to sorrel and use it as a vegetable, while others compare the taste to rhubarb and use it in desserts. I do both.

Because Japanese knotweed usually forms large thickets, it's easy to pick 5 or 6 pounds very quickly. That's enough for a batch of wine (page 236), syrup for cocktails (page 234), soup, pickles, stir-fries, and a couple of desserts.

If you simmer your Japanese knotweed stems in water, you'll notice something interesting: The stems turn dark green, while the water turns pink. Use the soft green stems to make a purée that can be used in cakes, and reserve the pink juice to make a simple syrup. It makes a great cocktail mixer, or it can be served as a mocktail with seltzer.

Japanese knotweed keeps for months in the freezer, and you don't need to blanch it first. You can use thawed Japanese knotweed for soups, wine, syrup, and purée, but pickles and stir-fries are better with fresh, snappy stems.

JAPANESE KNOTWEED
KNOW BEFORE YOU EAT

WHERE AND HOW TO FIND

- A perennial plant that prefers wet feet, but will also grow in soils with average moisture
- Look for last year's tall, dried, reddish-brown stalks; young spears will be at the base of old stalks.
- Grows well in sun or shade

ID CHECKLIST

- Often confused with bamboo, it has segmented stems and grows quickly.

- The more it grows in sun, the redder the variegation on the stems.

- Stems are hollow and may be ¼–1 inch in diameter (thickness is not an indication of tenderness or edibility).

- Stems may grow to be 10 feet tall but are more commonly 5–6 feet tall.

- Stems have a gentle curve at mature height.

- Leaves are oval, with pointed tips and smooth margins.

- Leaves are arranged alternately on the stem.

- Leaves may be 3–6 inches long and 2–4 inches wide.

- Small white flowers appear in late summer or early fall.

- Flowers are held on upright spikes originating from nodes on the upper part of the stem.

These stems are probably at the right stage for harvesting. Test them by trying to snap one off by hand.

These mature knotweed stems are not tasty.

Japanese knotweed produces copious amounts of flowers and seed.

SAMPHIRE

Salicornia species

A.k.a.: glasswort, sea bean, pickle weed, salt fingers, sea asparagus, chicken feet

Best part to eat: young stems and stem tips

When to harvest: whenever stems are tender

These plants are salt lovers, and they thrive where many plants won't grow at all. Samphire is succulent and actually looks cactuslike, which is weird, because it's a plant that prefers to keep its feet wet. Look for it along coastlines and in marshes. Some people cultivate samphire by growing it in containers they keep consistently moist and water with salt water.

Multiple species of samphire grow in the United States (and other places), and all of them can be used in the same way. Depending on where you forage, you may find sea glasswort (*Salicornia maritima*), common glasswort (*S. europaea*), and dwarf glasswort (*S. bigelovii*), among others.

HARVESTING

To harvest samphire, use scissors or pruners to snip off the top few inches of the plant. As the plant grows through the season, the stems can become woody lower down, but the tips should continue to be tender.

Samphire turns red as the growing season progresses. Saltiness may increase with variegation, so taste a bit before you harvest to see if it's too salty for you. Some of the salty flavor can be removed by soaking or blanching the harvest in unsalted water, but this will always be a salty plant.

Late in the season, samphire stems develop a woody core. If you find samphire late in the season and the stems are too woody to be eaten whole, do not despair! You can briefly boil the stems, then scrape off the green of the woody core. Combine the soft samphire pieces with pasta, rice, or potatoes to give them some zip.

Samphire can be either abundant or rare, depending on where you forage. If it's rare in your area, please leave some stem tips behind so the seeds (inedible) can ripen and produce a crop for the following year. You probably won't be able to see the flowers or seeds, but by leaving the tips of the plants in place you'll be leaving the reproductive parts behind.

Another thought about sustainability: Marshes and coastlands are decreasing as development increases. Samphire's habitat is threatened, so please keep this in mind as you harvest. Take only a small portion of what you find.

FEASTING

Some people compare samphire to asparagus, but this doesn't do justice to either plant. Samphire has much smaller, thinner stems than asparagus and the texture and flavor are completely different. I'm so tired of people saying every slim, upright stalk reminds them of asparagus. Use your imagination, people! It's hard to describe a new flavor in terms of a familiar one, so why bother to try? Just taste samphire and you'll see what I mean.

Samphire has salt water running through its veins! The sharpness of its flavor makes it an excellent accompaniment to fatty meats. It's a perfect side dish for ham, lamb, and Spam. (I couldn't resist the rhyme.) It's also commonly served with fish, perhaps because they are both water lovers. In Turkey it's a traditional vegetable, served steamed and dressed with olive oil, garlic, and lemon. No additional salt required.

If you're going to cook your samphire, be sure not to overdo it or it'll lose its characteristic crunch. Blanching for 1 to 2 minutes should do the trick, then shock your samphire in cold water to stop the cooking.

Samphire is also very tasty raw. Add it to salads (green, tuna, potato) and soups, or toss it in with pasta and parm.

Pickle weed is a common name that gives you another hint on how to use this plant. Pro tip: Don't use salt in your brine. This plant comes pre-salted.

Feeling experimental? You can dry and grind samphire to make your own foraged salt substitute.

WHERE AND HOW TO FIND

- A coastal plant that grows in marshy, salty mudflats and estuaries
- May be either annual or perennial, depending on the species
- Annual and perennial species come back in the same place year after year, as they reliably self-seed
- Full-sun plant

ID CHECKLIST

- Succulent upright foliage looks sculptural sticking up out of mud or marshy water.
- Stems are divided into segments, stacked on top of each other.
- Stems branch freely.
- Leaves look like bumps at each stem node.
- Plants grow to be about 12–15 inches tall.
- Stems are approximately ¼ inch in diameter.
- Tiny flowers are neither pretty nor tasty.
- Stems take on a reddish tint at the end of the growing season (not a reliable indicator of saltiness).
- Taste before you harvest in quantity.

tender, young, salty shoots

Samphire takes on a red color at the end of the growing season.

VIRGINIA WATERLEAF

Hydrophyllum virginianum

A.k.a.: eastern waterleaf, Appalachian waterleaf, Shawnee salad, John's cabbage

Best part to eat: leaves

When to harvest: any time, but tastiest in spring

Many references say that the young leaves of Virginia waterleaf are splotched with white, and that subsequent leaves are solid green. The common name is taken from the leaf splotches that someone, somewhere thought looked like water stains on the leaves. However, I have on multiple occasions found the earliest spring leaves of Virginia waterleaf to be entirely without splotches. (I have evidence!) So if you're just learning this plant, please don't consider the splotches to be a reliable identification characteristic.

Virginia waterleaf is an aggressive grower, so it's unlikely you'll put a dent in the population by harvesting for supper. Still, it isn't abundant in all locations (like my home state of New Hampshire), so remember to leave some behind.

FEASTING

So many greens have similar flavors, but Virginia waterleaf stands out for the hint of natural sweetness in its young foliage. It's a mild green, and some call it bland. Bitter greens are great, but it's all about balance, and there's a place for mild greens in the kitchen. I don't know why more people don't appreciate Virginia waterleaf; I'm quite fond of the young leaves.

Not all waterleaf foliage has white variegation.

Virginia waterleaf is a versatile green. It's good for using raw in salads in early spring or as a cooked green later in the season. If the hairs on the leaves bother you, cooking will make them magically disappear. Cooked leaves can be used instead of spinach in quiches, stir-fries, soups, and stews.

Virginia waterleaf leaves may (or may not) become bitter with age. Plants growing in sun are more likely to become bitter, so sample a leaf or two before harvesting in summer or fall.

LOOK-ALIKES

Some foragers confuse Virginia waterleaf with ground elder (*Aegopodium podagraria*), which is also edible. (Ground elder also goes by the common names goutweed, bishop's weed, and many others.) They do look somewhat alike, and both are often found in vast swaths. The flowers of these two plants are very different, however. Ground elder has flat clusters of small white flowers held high above the plant, similar to those of Queen Anne's lace (page 96). The flavor of ground elder is stronger than that of Virginia waterleaf and resembles that of celery.

Virginia waterleaf also looks remarkably like sochan (page 107), another edible green. Sochan doesn't have the variegation that Virginia waterleaf sometimes has, and since it's also edible, you won't make a fatal mistake if you get confused.

ground elder

sochan

VIRGINIA WATERLEAF
KNOW BEFORE YOU EAT

WHERE AND HOW TO FIND

- A perennial plant, it will return to the same place year after year.
- Native habitat is shady woodlands with moist soils
- Has an aggressive growth habit and may form large colonies (beautiful in bloom)
- East Coast species, but similar species found west of the Mississippi

ID CHECKLIST

- Plants appear in early spring, at about the same time as garlic mustard.
- Foliage is highly variable, both from plant to plant, and throughout the growing season.
- Leaves may be solid green or splotched with white variegation; variegation may change over time.
- Foliage shape is distinctive, with three to seven lobes per leaf; a single plant may have leaves with varying numbers of lobes.
- Leaves are usually coarsely toothed.
- Foliage becomes slightly fuzzy with age.
- Foliage hairs are pretty much undetectable in early spring.
- Leaves alternate along the stem and are approximately 6–8 inches long.
- Plants grow to be 12–24 inches tall.

- Stems may be flushed with purple at leaf nodes.
- Bell-shaped flowers may be shades of blue and purple, or white.
- Flowers have five petals, five sepals, and five very prominent stamens.
- Flowers appear in May–August, depending on where you forage.
- Flowers are borne in clusters approximately 2 inches in diameter.
- Individual flowers are 1/4–1/2 inch wide.
- Edible flowers are more decorative than delicious; they look nice sprinkled on a salad.
- Plants may die back over summer in hot, dry conditions.

The white variegation makes it easier to identify Virginia waterleaf, but it's not always present.

WATERCRESS

Nasturtium officinale

A.k.a.: *Rorippa nasturtium-aquaticum*, water radish

Best part to eat: leaves and stems

When to harvest: any time

I love watercress. It has great flavor and it's super nutritious and extremely versatile, with a very long season. You can often forage for it in the middle of winter, as long as the water it grows in hasn't frozen.

Watercress is an aquatic plant with lightweight, hollow stems that allow it to float. It spreads easily, often covering a stream for an acre or more, and it's shallow-rooted, so you can dig up a few plants and transplant them to your very own, cool, slow-moving stream at home. Watercress needs to grow in moving water in order to thrive.

Watercress is in the mustard family (Brassicaceae), along with familiar vegetables like broccoli and Brussels sprouts. Like most members of this plant family, it has a strong flavor. Its stems and leaves have a sharp peppery taste, reminiscent of horseradish but less harsh.

HARVESTING

If you're planning to harvest, not transplant, watercress, don't pull it up by the roots. Simply snip the stems off just above water level, or pinch off the stems with your fingers. The plant is quite tender and easy to harvest with your bare hands. The leaves, flowers, and stems are all edible.

Wild watercress isn't safe to eat raw. If the water that the cress grows in contains animal waste, it may also contain parasites like the liver fluke. These parasites can take up residence in the human liver and the consequences aren't pretty. If you plan to cook the watercress, no problem. Boiling the plant for a few minutes kills the parasite and renders it harmless. If you have your heart set on a raw watercress salad, you have a few options. You can soak the plants in water with iodine tablets (the kind used by backpackers to purify drinking

Watercress grows best in cool, slow-moving streams.

water), or you can pick the stem above the water level. Here's how that works.

The stage of the liver fluke that lives on water plants is immobile (encysted). It lives on the underwater part of the plant and cannot climb up the watercress. As a dicot, watercress grows from its tips, not from the base of the plant. In other words, the underwater part stays underwater, unless the water level in your stream drops significantly. So, if you're in the middle of a drought and the stream is lower than usual, play it safe with your watercress, and either cook it or soak in an iodine solution. But if the water level is consistent, and you harvest from an inch or two above water level, your raw watercress should be fluke free.

Don't do anything that doesn't feel safe to you. Cooked watercress is delicious, and if you only eat it that way, that's swell. I've found watercress in places where I wouldn't be comfortable eating it raw. I also have a clean, reliable watercress spot, and when I harvest there, I feel safe eating that cress raw.

FEASTING

The assertive flavor of watercress lends itself to many dishes. It's superb in a delicate tea sandwich on crustless bread with a skim of sweet butter. It spices up a green salad, and nicely offsets the taste of sweet ingredients like fruit or cultivated lettuces. Watercress soup can be served hot, cold, or room temperature, and watercress elevates vichyssoise to a whole new level of deliciousness.

Make a peppery watercress pesto for bruschetta, pasta, or to stir into risotto. Infuse your favorite olive oil with the color and flavor of watercress. Make a watercress sauce to serve with chicken or fish. I don't mean to sound bossy, but there are a lot of good ways to use watercress and you should try them all.

WHERE AND HOW TO FIND

- Grows in cool, slow-moving water
- Look in streams, and in lakes and ponds if there's lots of water movement.
- Perennial plant, so you'll find it in the same place year after year
- Grows in sun or shade
- Look for thick green mats of foliage floating on top of moving water.

ID CHECKLIST

- Foliage is 3–6 inches long.
- Each leaf is divided into 5–11 oval leaflets.
- Terminal leaflet on each leaf is larger than the other leaflets.
- Leaves are medium to dark green and alternate.
- Small white flowers (approximately ¼ inch in diameter) are borne in terminal clusters.
- Flowers are four-petaled (characteristic of mustard family).

- Roots grow in mud at the bottoms of streams.
- Foliage is mostly held above water level, although part of the stem and some leaves may be below water level.
- Stems are round, smooth, and hollow.
- Plants may grow to be 12–14 inches tall, but much of the growth may be underwater.

Watercress flowers are also edible.

WINTERCRESS

Barbarea vulgaris

A.k.a.: yellow rocketcress, rocketcress, bittercress, creasy greens

Best part to eat: young leaves, immature flower buds

When to harvest: early spring

This is a bitter green. If you appreciate bitter flavors (like radicchio) and/or vegetables in the broccoli family (like arugula and broccoli rabe), wintercress may be for you.

Wintercress is one of the earliest wild greens to forage. It's a cool-weather wild edible, with texture and flavor being most pleasant in spring and in fall. The greens, immature flower buds, mature flowers, and seeds are edible.

Wintercress tolerates a range of soil types (from sandy to clay), but it appreciates regular moisture. It can be found in drier soils, but the plant will be smaller and tougher, with less lush foliage. It's easiest to spot in bloom, covered with the bright yellow flowers typical of so many members of the mustard family. Each flower has four petals arranged in an uneven cross. There are six stamens in the middle of each flower: two short, four long. This flower structure is a key identification factor for all members of the mustard family.

Wintercress is a biennial or winter annual, depending on where it grows. First-year leaves form a basal rosette of foliage, and second-year plants flower and set seed. If the seeds of wintercress germinate the year they fall to the ground (this will depend on the climate), they will produce their basal rosette that same year, then flower the next year, and are thus considered a winter annual. If seeds germinate the year after they fall, they form the basal rosette in year one, and the flower stalk in year two. This is the more common growth habit, and this is why most people consider the plant a biennial.

FEASTING

Because wintercress is a bitter green, it needs a little help to make it palatable for most people. The easiest thing to do is to combine wintercress greens with mild greens like chickweed, nettles (pages 184 and 188), or Virginia waterleaf (page 210) to create a balanced dish.

Leaves. If you want to try wintercress raw on its own, you can soak it for 30 minutes in ice water to remove some (not all) of the bitterness, or massage the leaves by rubbing them between your fingers until they feel wilted. If you've never heard of a leaf massage, try this experiment: Take two similar leaves from the same plant and rub one between your fingers until it feels wilted. Take a bite from each leaf and compare the flavors.

There are other ways to mellow the flavor of bitter greens, and all of them work well with wintercress.

- Briefly blanch wintercress in several changes of water, but don't let the greens turn to mush. Do this without the lid on the pot to allow the bitter compounds to escape along with the steam.

- Cook bitter greens with strong flavors like cured meat, strong cheese, garlic, or hot peppers.

- Add acids like vinegar and citrus to help balance bitter flavors.

- Apply salt to mellow bitter flavors. The salt can come from many sources such as preserved lemons, feta cheese, or anchovies. Plain old sea salt works, too.

- Add fats like butter, cream, and cheese to temper bitterness.

Buds. The immature flower buds are best used the same way you'd use broccoli rabe. Blanch the buds briefly (30 to 60 seconds), then add them to quiches and omelets, or serve them with pasta.

Flowers. Add open flowers to salads, pasta, and rice dishes. The flowers are less bitter than the rest of the plant, but you should still taste them before using them. People have widely varying senses of taste, and what's pleasantly bitter to some may be overpowering to others.

Seeds. Ripe seeds are small and probably not worth your while, but they can be used to make your own wild mustard or simply ground and used as a spice.

WINTERCRESS
KNOW BEFORE YOU EAT

WHERE AND HOW TO FIND

- An early spring green, it sometimes emerges before the snow has completely melted.

- Tolerates a wide range of soils (sand to gravel to clay) but grows best with regular moisture

- Grows in sun or shade

- Easiest to spot when in full bloom although this isn't the best time to harvest the leaves, which may be too bitter and fibrous to be tasty

- Reseeds itself, so you'll usually find it in the same spot year after year

- Grows in 43 of the lower 48 states

ID CHECKLIST

- Herbaceous biennial grows to be approximately 2–3 feet tall
- Shiny, dark green basal rosette of foliage the first year
- First-year leaves are 2–8 inches long, lobed, with the terminal lobe being considerably larger than the side lobes.
- Second-year growth produces a flower stem that eventually branches and produces multiple flower buds.
- Flower stalk leaves are smaller, and the lobes are narrower, than basal leaves.
- Leaves on the flower stalk are arranged alternately and clasp the stalk directly; they do not have leaf stems.
- Flower stalks have obvious ridges.
- Yellow flowers have four petals arranged in an uneven cross and six stamens: two short, four long.

Note the larger terminal leaf lobe.

Leaves on the flower stalk clasp the stalk directly.

Flowers make the plant easy to identify, but at this stage the foliage is too bitter to enjoy.

CHAPTER 6

PRESERVING THE HARVEST

As every forager knows, wild edible harvests are intensely seasonal. Some examples: You've got 2 or 3 weeks (max) to harvest black raspberries. Nettles must be picked before they flower. And once Japanese knotweed turns woody, it's useless to you in the kitchen. No one is flying in any wild edibles from the Southern Hemisphere and stocking them in grocery stores to tide us over in winter, so if you want to enjoy your foraged harvests year-round, you'll need to learn how to preserve them when they're at their peak.

Kitchen Tools

Having the right tool for any job makes your work easier, and if something is easier to do, you'll do it more often!

DEHYDRATOR

If you have an oven that you can set to very low temperatures (125°F/50°C), you may not need a dehydrator. But most ovens don't have settings that go below 170°F (75°C), which is too high for dehydrating most foraged harvests. Depending on the model, dehydrators can be set for anywhere from 90 to 150°F (30 to 65°C). Lower temperatures are best for preserving flavor, so I dry almost everything at 95°F (35°C). Dehydrators use less energy than stoves and many have timers, making them very convenient. Special nonstick sheets (for making fruit leather) can be ordered to fit the dehydrating trays.

SPICE GRINDER

Yes, you could chop your spices with a knife or grind them with a mortar and pestle. I prefer a coffee bean grinder to grind fresh, dried, and frozen spices. Of course I don't grind coffee beans in this grinder; their strong taste would carry over to the spices. The spices have their own dedicated grinder.

JELLY BAG AND STAND

You can certainly strain fruit juice using a colander lined with cheesecloth, but I prefer a dedicated jelly bag. Jelly bags are reusable, which is nice. Also, they are long and narrow, so the stacked weight of the fruit makes for faster juice extraction.

FOOD MILL

A food mill lets you quickly separate seeds, stems, and skin from your fruit harvests. It also makes it easy to purée. Look for a food mill with several plates with different-size holes. The smaller the hole, the more muscle you'll need to turn the mill, so you'll want to use the plate with the largest possible hole that will still catch the seeds, while letting the pulp and juice pass through.

STEAM JUICER

This may not be an essential kitchen tool for everyone, but if you're going to be juicing lots of foraged fruits, it can be a real labor saver. A steam juicer has three parts: On the bottom is a solid pan that holds water; in the middle is a section that resembles a Bundt pan, with a cutout in the middle (this pan also has an outlet to which a piece of translucent tubing is attached); and on the top is a pan that is partially perforated on the sides and bottom.

The beauty of a steam juicer is that the steam does all the work. You fill the bottom pan about three-quarters of the way with water, place the empty middle pan on top of that, then place the top pan on top of the middle pan, and fill it with fruit. As steam rises, it breaks open the skins of the fruit and the juice drips through the perforations into the middle pan where it collects until you release it through the tube into a collection vessel.

CANNING JARS

Whether you're pressure canning or canning in a boiling water bath, you'll need special jars with two-part lids that create a vacuum seal to keep your food safe.

BOILING WATER BATH CANNER

If you're only going to make a few jars of jam or jelly every year, you probably don't need a dedicated canner. You can process pint or half-pint jars in a large pasta pot. Put a folded-up dish towel on the bottom of the pot so the jars don't crack while they're jostling around in the boiling water, and be sure the water covers the tops of your jars by 2 inches. For larger jars you may need to buy a dedicated water bath canner. These can accommodate quart jars and come with a rack that makes it easy to lift the jars in and out of the boiling water.

PRESSURE CANNER

While jams, jellies, and pickles can be canned in a boiling water bath, low acid foods like foraged greens need to be pressure canned to be safe. This is not the same thing as a pressure cooker, which is intended to cook foods under pressure faster than you'd be able to cook them normally. You can use a pressure canner for pressure cooking but not always vice versa. Most pressure cookers are too small to accommodate the height of pint and quart jars.

HIGH-POWERED BLENDER

A quality blender makes short work of grinding flour. You can do small batches in a spice grinder, but if you want to make large quantities of flour (such as from acorns), this is the tool for the job. It's also great for making smoothies, ice cream and sorbet, and purées.

PRESERVING TECHNIQUES

DRYING

Dehydration is one of the easiest and least expensive ways to preserve your herbs and fruits. If you had a banner year for wild garlic or cranberries, why not fill your pantry with jars of dried wild produce?

My favorite way to dry a harvest is with a dehydrator. Mine has paid for itself many times over. You don't have to buy new. Search through the classified ads on websites like Craigslist, and you might just find one for a fraction of its original retail price.

If you live someplace humid, a dehydrator is essential for drying herbs and fruit. High humidity can cause these foods to mold before they dry. Herbs are best dried at 95°F (35°C) or lower. This is because volatile oils, which contain most of the flavor, are preserved at lower temperatures. Fruit and fruit leather can be dried at 135°F (55°C). Look for a dehydrator with a thermostat so you can adjust the temperature to suit what you're drying. A timer is also a nice bonus.

Of course you can dry food without a dehydrator. If you live someplace arid, try a double screen setup. Place your herbs (or fruits) on one screen, then cover with a second screen on top. The mesh allows air to circulate from above and below, and it protects your harvest from pilfering birds and mammals.

Several companies make screened, collapsible shelves you can hang in a breezy spot. Drying in open air usually keeps the temperature below 95°F (35°C). Maintaining a low temperature with this method may be a challenge in truly hot desert locales, such as Phoenix or Death Valley. Depending on the humidity where you live, it may take several days for your harvest to dry.

If you don't have an equipment budget, you can always bundle your harvest and hang it in a dry, dark place. But don't be fooled by those pretty magazine photos of kitchens bedecked with colorful bundles of herbs. Dried herbs left in a working kitchen will quickly become dusty and lose their flavor. Once your harvests have dried, transfer them to sealed containers and store them in a dark place to preserve their color and flavor.

Oven and microwave drying are a last resort. Most traditional ovens can't be set below 170°F (75°C), which is too high for herbs and even higher than I'd recommend for fruits and fruit leather. But we make the best of what we've got, right? Prop open the door of your oven with a wooden spoon to lower the internal oven temperature. Try not to think about the energy you're wasting.

Microwaves can be used to dry herbs, but not for fruit. As with a traditional oven, you'll lose some flavor due to the high temperature, but at least you won't be heating your house with an open oven. Place your herbs in a single layer on a dry paper towel, and microwave at full power for 30-second intervals until the herbs are crisp. Replace the paper towel if it becomes wet, and be sure to let your herbs cool before you transfer them to a jar. Condensation may form during cooldown, which could lead to mold.

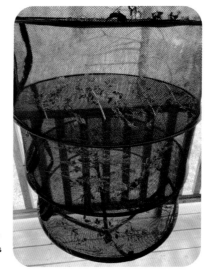

This multitiered, screened-in air dryer lets you dry loads of herbs without electricity.

BLANCHING AND FREEZING

While some foragers dry and powder their greens, I do not. I suppose you could add powdered greens to soups or stews as a thickener, but you lose a lot of flavor and all the texture this way, which is a crying shame. Blanching and freezing is the best way to preserve your harvest of leaves and stems, as this process maintains both the color and nutrition of the plants you've picked. And thanks to Harold McGee and his fantastic book *On Food and Cooking*, I can explain exactly why blanching and freezing works so well.

Freezing your greens stops their metabolic processes. When the water in plant tissue freezes, it becomes immobile, and this, in turn, immobilizes most other molecules in the plant, causing most chemical activity to come to a screeching halt.

Ah, but some chemical reactions are actually enhanced by freezing. The formation of ice crystals speeds up the enzymatic breakdown of both pigments and vitamins by concentrating the enzymes

and other molecules responsible for these processes. As a result, your frozen food will thaw to be less beautiful and less nutritious than when it was fresh.

Here's where the blanching comes in. Blanching stops the enzymatic breakdown of pigments and vitamins. To blanch your greens, bring a large pot of water to a rolling boil, and plunge your greens into the water. How long you blanch your greens will depend on how thick they are. Milkweed shoots may need a full 2 minutes, while quickweed leaves could be done in 30 seconds. You'll develop a feel for this with experience. Strain the greens and transfer them to a bowl of ice water to stop the cooking. Overcook your greens and you'll be left with mush. Undercook, and your frozen greens will end up a dull color with fewer nutrients.

Once your greens have completely cooled, squeeze out as much water as possible from the leaves to minimize the accumulation of ice crystals in the plant tissue. These sharp crystals puncture the plant's cell walls and destroy the structure of the plant, once again leaving you with mush.

If you plan to freeze your greens long term (more than a few weeks), use a vacuum sealer to package them. Removing the air is crucial. Because water seeks equilibrium, and because the air in your freezer is very cold and dry, without a vacuum seal, ice crystals in frozen food will evaporate. This results in freezer burn, which produces a stale flavor and tough texture.

Remember how hard you worked to harvest your nettles, dock, and mustard greens? Surely you don't want all that effort to go to waste. The extra steps of blanching before freezing, then tightly packaging your greens and removing as much air as possible with a vacuum sealer, are worth the time it takes to preserve your harvest at its peak.

FREEZING WITHOUT BLANCHING

Some things can be frozen without blanching, primarily fruits and nuts. I often freeze acorns immediately after gathering them, because I don't have time to process them right away. And while fruits like plums and crabapples can certainly be canned, it's a lot easier and a lot less laborious to toss them in the freezer.

Nuts don't require any prep work before freezing. Just put them in a freezer bag, shells and all, and store them away. Thaw them when you have time to play with your harvest.

Fruit should be rinsed and dried before freezing. If you're going to use the fruit in jam or jelly, you can freeze it in a ziplock bag, or vacuum seal it if it's going to be a few months before you get around to using it. If you're freezing berries to use in baking, and you want the original shape and texture of the fruit to be preserved, consider spreading them in a single layer on a cookie sheet (after you've rinsed and dried them), then put them in the freezer. After they're frozen, transfer the berries to a freezer bag or vacuum seal them. If you just toss them in a bag after rinsing and drying, you will likely have a giant mass of fruit pulp, which is fine for some things but not for others.

CANNING

If you decide to make a deep dive into food preservation, you may want to consider investing in a boiling water bath canner, a pressure canner, or both. The nice thing about canned goods is that you don't have to wait for them to defrost, and they can be stored anywhere (under the bed, at the back of the closet, and of course, in a kitchen cupboard).

Jams, jellies, syrups, and pickles can all be canned in a boiling water bath, which is basically a big stockpot. This type of canning is only for high-acid foods, foods with added sugar, or pickled foods.

A pressure canner can be used to can any kind of food, including greens, roots, and fruit, without additional sweetener. Pressure canning will give you a soft (dare I say mushy?) end product, but if you're just going to use the canned greens as a soup base, it really doesn't make a difference. Check out *Put 'em Up!* or *The Beginner's Guide to Preserving Food at Home* for detailed canning instructions.

TECHNIQUES FOR MAKING PANTRY STAPLES

Naturally Fermented Soda

This technique takes advantage of the natural yeasts found in many flower pollens. Ratios of 3:1 (water:sugar) and 2:1 (water:loosely packed flowers) generally work well for this technique. For example, for 12 cups of water you would need 4 cups of sugar and 6 cups of loosely packed flowers. You'll also need one thinly sliced lemon or lime for every 12 cups of water.

INGREDIENTS

- Flowers
- Sugar
- Water
- Thinly sliced lemon or lime

MATERIALS

- Food-grade bucket
- Dish towel
- Large rubber band
- Sanitized plastic bottles

1. Inspect your flowers and shake off any insects. Don't rinse the blooms or you'll wash away those naturally occurring yeasts before they can work their magic. Snip off the individual flowers and transfer them to a food-grade bucket large enough to accommodate the liquid.

2. Combine the sugar and water in a large pot, and whisk to dissolve the sugar.

3. Pour the sugar-water solution over the flowers, add the citrus slices, and stir. Cover the top of the bucket with a dish towel and fasten with a rubber band. Leave the bucket on your kitchen counter.

4. Remove the dish towel once a day and give the brew a stir. When fermentation begins you'll see bubbles after you stir. How soon this happens will depend on the temperature of your home and the amount of natural yeasts present. It may take 2 days, or it may take a week. Start tasting 5 days after fermentation begins and see if you like the flavor. If it tastes too yeasty, let it sit a few more days.

5. When the flavor suits your taste, strain off the solids and bottle your brew, leaving a few inches at the top of each bottle. I suggest using recycled plastic bottles for this so you can feel when the gas produced by fermentation needs to be released.

6. Keep the bottles in a cool, dark place for about a week, where the liquid will continue to ferment, producing carbon dioxide. This builds up pressure in the bottles and forces the gas to dissolve into the liquid. The pressurized gas will be released as fizzy bubbles when the bottle is opened. Check the bottles every day, and when they feel very firm, release some gas to relieve the pressure.

7. Move the bottles to the refrigerator and enjoy. Because these natural sodas have no preservatives, they should be drunk within a week or two.

Flower Syrup

Any strongly scented, edible flower will make a flavorful syrup. As with the naturally fermented soda recipe (page 232), don't wash your flower petals; pollen and yeast contribute to the flavor.

You'll need equal parts fragrant flower petals, white sugar, and water. You can use other sweeteners, but white sugar has a very neutral flavor, which keeps the focus on the flavor of the flower.

INGREDIENTS

- Flower petals
- White sugar
- Water

MATERIALS

- Bowl
- Plastic wrap
- Saucepan
- Jar with tight-fitting lid

1. Combine the flower petals and sugar in a bowl and mix well. Cover the bowl with plastic wrap or a lid, and let it sit overnight.

2. Move the sugar and petals to a saucepan and add the water. Place over medium heat and whisk to dissolve the sugar. Rub the liquid between your fingers. When you can't feel the sugar grains, remove the saucepan from the heat. Cover and let it sit overnight.

3. Strain off the flower petals, pressing them to remove as much liquid as possible. Transfer the syrup to a jar with a tight-fitting lid. This flower syrup will keep for several months in the refrigerator.

Vinegar

Vinegar has a strong flavor all on its own, so if you want to infuse it with something wild, choose a plant with a taste that can stand up to the vinegar. Some things to try are melilot flowers, wild garlic stems, Pennsylvania bay leaves, or sumac berries. Bright red sumac fruit will give you a lovely colored vinegar.

INGREDIENTS

- ¼ cup diced strong-flavored herbs
- 2 cups white vinegar

MATERIALS

- 1-pint canning jar
- Jar or bottle with tight-fitting lid

Combine the herbs with the white vinegar in a pint jar. Allow the mixture to infuse for about 2 weeks, then strain off the solids and transfer the vinegar to your jar.

Wine

Fermentation requires yeast, and yeast requires food in the form of sugars. Because different wild plants contain different amounts of sugar, the exact proportions you use to make a wild wine depend on the foraged ingredient. The recipe below is for a simple crabapple wine. For an excellent collection of wild wine recipes, I recommend Making Wild Wines & Meads *by Pattie Vargas and Rich Gulling.*

INGREDIENTS

- 4 pounds crabapples
- 1 gallon water
- 3 pounds sugar
- 1 package commercial wine yeast (not bread yeast!)

MATERIALS

- 2-gallon food-grade bucket
- Jelly bag or cheesecloth
- 1-gallon glass jug
- Fermentation lock or balloon with hole prick
- Wine bottles

1. Roughly chop the crabapples and put them in the bucket.

2. Combine the water and sugar in a large pot. Bring the water to a boil and stir to dissolve the sugar.

3. Pour the sugar-water over the chopped fruit. Cover the bucket and let it sit for 24 hours.

4. Add the yeast, stir, and re-cover the bucket. Stir daily for 1 week.

5. Strain off the solids through a jelly bag or a cheesecloth-lined colander and transfer the liquid to a gallon glass jug with a fermentation lock or a balloon with a hole pricked in it. This allows the fermentation gasses to escape and will keep out fruit flies and other insects.

6. Most wild wines need to mature for at least a year, but check your jug every few months. Any time you see about ½ inch of solids in the bottom of the jug, rack the wine by pouring off the liquid and disposing of the solids. When very little sediment is produced, bottle your wine.

Fruit-Infused Spirits

You can infuse any kind of spirit with any kind of fruit. But the neutral flavor of vodka allows the foraged ingredient to shine, so let's start there. The technique is the same for any spirit you may use.

Sweet fruits like bramble berries don't need any sweetener, but if you're using a tart fruit, like plums or chokecherries, you may want to add some sugar to the mix. The amount depends on the fruit. Start small and increase until the flavor pleases you.

INGREDIENTS

- 3 cups roughly chopped fruit
- 750 ml vodka
- ½–1 cup sugar or more to taste (optional)

MATERIALS

- 1-gallon canning jar
- 750 ml bottle

1. For a simple infusion, transfer the fruit to a large container with a lid (a 1-gallon canning jar is perfect). If you're using sugar, add it now.

2. Pour the contents of a 750 ml bottle of vodka (save the bottle) over the fruit, shake well, and put it somewhere on your kitchen counter.

3. Give the jar a shake once a day, and taste after 2 weeks. If you like the flavor, great. If you want a stronger fruit flavor, let it sit another week.

4. Strain off the solids and return the flavored spirit to its original bottle.

Jelly

To make jelly, you need to get fruit juice to jell, which requires pectin. Some fruits (wild plums, cranberries, crabapples) contain enough pectin to jell on their own. But for jellies made with low-pectin fruit (raspberries, rose hips, sumac), you'll need to add commercial pectin. If you're not sure which way to go, err on the side of caution and add the pectin. You'll find recipes and instructions on the insert in the pectin package. You can also make jelly by adding commercial pectin to an infusion of flower petals, like Queen Anne's lace, dandelions, or rose petals. The following recipe is for making fruit jelly without commercial pectin.

INGREDIENTS

- Fruit
- Water
- Sugar
- Lemon juice

MATERIALS

- Shallow pan
- Jelly bag or cheesecloth
- Metal spoon
- Jars

1. Juice your fruit. Place your fruit in a shallow pan and barely cover with water. Bring the water to a boil, then reduce heat and simmer until the fruit is soft. Mash the fruit, then pour it (and the accompanying liquid) through a jelly bag or several layers of cheesecloth. Allow the liquid to drip for several hours. Don't squeeze the bag or you may get a cloudy jelly. Nobody likes a cloudy jelly.

2. Measure the juice and transfer it to your shallow pan. For each cup of juice, add ¾ cup of sugar and 1 tablespoon of lemon juice. Don't process more than 4 cups of juice at a time. Why? The short explanation is that it could mess with the formation of the ever-important pectin bond.

Your jelly has reached the jelling point when the last two drops slide together, and drip from the spoon as a single drop.

3. Bring the mixture to a boil, whisking regularly. When the bubbles become small and regular and the juice takes on a glossy finish, start testing for the jelling point. To do this, use a metal spoon to scoop up a spoonful of liquid and hold it over your jelly pan with the bowl of the spoon at a 90-degree angle to the liquid. Watch the juice drip off the spoon. The drops become progressively thicker as the jelly cooks. When the last two drops from the spoon slide together to form a single drop (as opposed to dripping off the spoon as two separate drops) you have reached the jelling point. Turn off the heat.

4. Transfer your jelly into jars, and either refrigerate or water bath can for long-term preservation.

Infusing Cream

Many flowers infuse wonderfully in cream, adding surprising flavor to the rich liquid. The same technique can be used for herbs.

INGREDIENTS

- Cream
- Flower petals

MATERIALS

- Heavy saucepan
- Strainer

1. In a heavy saucepan, combine equal parts cream and loosely packed flower petals.

2. Heat the liquid gently, whisking occasionally to avoid scorching. When bubbles begin to appear around the edge of the saucepan, reduce the heat and simmer for 25 minutes, stirring regularly. Do not boil the cream!

3. When the time is up, strain the cream with a strainer, throw away the flowers, and use the infused cream to make ice cream, panna cotta, or any other cream-based delicacy your heart desires.

GLOSSARY

annual: a plant that lives for 1 year, growing from seed to flower to seed, then dying

anther: the pollen-bearing part of the stamen

biennial: a plant that lives for 2 years, producing leaves the first year, then flowering, producing seed, and dying the second year

blanch: to quickly boil in water, usually for 1 to 2 minutes

bract: a leaf- or petal-like structure surrounding a flower

bulb: underground storage organ that is part of the root system of some plants

bulbil: a small secondary bulb that forms between a leaf and stem, or in place of flowers

calyx: the collective term for sepals

compound leaf: a leaf composed of more than one part

cultivar: a single, manmade genetic representation of a species or hybrid

deciduous: a plant that loses its leaves for part of the year, usually in winter

disc flowers: the upright, tubular flowers found in the central part of compound flowers in the sunflower family; usually surrounded by ray flowers

disturbed soil: soil that has been disturbed by cultivation, construction, clearing, or other actions, leaving the soil surface open to settlement by plants

elliptical leaf: a leaf shaped like an ellipse, that is, broadest in the middle

evergreen: a plant that maintains green foliage throughout the year

filament: the stalk that bears the anther

genus: a group of plants classified together due to common ancestry; plural = genera

growth habit: the shape or form of a plant; the speed with which a plant grows

herbaceous: a plant lacking woody growth above ground

hybridize: to interbreed between two species (or sometimes genera) of plants

invasive plant: a non-native plant with an aggressive growth habit that interferes with normal growth in an ecosystem

lanceolate leaf: a lance-shaped leaf with the widest part at the base

leach: to remove a chemical substance with water

leaf axil: where the leaf joins the stem

leaflet: a segment of a compound leaf

lenticel: a raised mark on a woody plant stem that allows for gas exchange between the atmosphere and interior plant tissue

meristematic growth: tender, new plant growth where plant cells are dividing and reproducing rapidly, usually at the tips of roots and shoots

mucilage: slimy, thick substance

ocrea: a sheath at the base of a leaf

ovary: contains the ovule (seed) and eventually becomes the wall of the fruit produced by the plant

overwinter: to live through the winter

ovule: contains the egg cell and becomes the seed

palmate: a leaf with leaflets, lobes, and veins originating from a center point, like fingers from a palm

pectin: a water-soluble carbohydrate found in plant cells that is often extracted to use as a gelling agent in jams and jellies

perennial: a plant that lives for more than 2 years, setting seeds multiple times

petiole: the stem of a leaf

pinnate: a leaf with leaflets arranged along a central stem

pistil: collectively the female parts of a flower, including the stigma, style, and ovary

prickles: sharp projections from the epidermis (outer layer of cells) of a plant

ray flowers: often called petals, these are actually flowers that surround the disc flowers of plants in the sunflower family

rhizome: an underground, horizontal stem that produces both roots and shoots

rosette: a ring of leaves, usually at the base of a plant

seed head: the structure that holds the seeds of a plant after flowering

self-seed: to disperse seeds without the help of humans, animals, or insects

sepal: the outer whorl of a flower, collectively the calyx; may resemble leaves or petals

spatulate: shaped like a spatula

species: a further division of a genus; a closely related group of plants

stamen: collectively the male parts of a flower, including the filament and anther

stigma: the top part of the pistil that receives the pollen

stolon: an above-ground horizontal stem that produces both roots and shoots

straight species: the native species of a plant before it has been hybridized, either by nature or by human intervention

style: the tube that connects the stigma to the ovary

tannin: a bitter-tasting organic compound found in some plant tissues

taproot: a thick, vertical, primary root

terminal cluster of flowers: a cluster of flowers at the end (terminus) of a branch or stem

RESOURCES

Want to know more? (You know you do.) Here's where you can explore online or in old-fashioned books (still my favorite way to read).

BOOKS

Barstow, Stephen, *Around the World in 80 Plants*. Permanent Publications, 2015.

Berglund, Berndt and Clare E. Bolsby, *The Edible Wild*. Scribner, 1971.

Cohen, Russ, *Wild Plants I Have Known . . . and Eaten*. Essex County Greenbelt Association, 2004.

Couplan, François, *The Encyclopedia of Edible Plants of North America*. Keats Publishing, 1998.

Elpel, Thomas and Kris Reed, *Foraging the Mountain West*. Hops Press, 2014.

Gibbons, Euell, *Stalking the Wild Asparagus*. Stackpole Books, 2020.

Kallas, John, *Edible Wild Plants*. Gibbs Smith, 2010.

Kindscher, Kelly, *Edible Wild Plants of the Prairie*. University Press of Kansas, 1987.

Lincoff, Gary, *The Joy of Foraging*. Crestline Books, 2017.

Meredith, Leda, *The Forager's Feast*. Countryman Press, 2016.

Meredith, Leda, *The Skillful Forager*. Roost Books, 2019.

Regional Foraging series from Timber Press, various authors.

Thayer, Samuel, *The Forager's Harvest*. Foragers Harvest Press, 2006.

Thayer, Samuel, *Incredible Wild Edibles*. Foragers Harvest Press, 2017.

Thayer, Samuel, *Nature's Garden*. Foragers Harvest Press, 2010.

Vorderbruggen, Mark, *Foraging* (Idiot's Guides). Alpha, 2016.

Zachos, Ellen, *Backyard Foraging*. Storey Publishing, 2013.

Zachos, Ellen, *The Forager's Pantry*. Gibbs Smith, 2021.

Zachos, Ellen, *The Wildcrafted Cocktail*. Storey Publishing, 2021.

WEBSITES

Backyard Forager
https://backyardforager.com

Eat the Weeds
https://eattheweeds.com

Edible Leeds
https://edible-leeds
.blogspot.com

Foraging Texas
https://foragingtexas.com

Galloway Wild Foods
https://gallowaywildfoods.com

Hunger and Thirst
https://hungerandthirstforlife
.blogspot.com

The 3 Foragers
https://the3foragers
.blogspot.com

Wild Food Girl
https://wildfoodgirl.com

INDEX

Page numbers in *italics* indicate photos.

A

acorns
  feasting on, 140
  harvesting, 139–140, *139*
  leaching/storing, 141–42
Aegopodium podagraria. See ground elder
aggressive edible plants, 16
allergies, 12, 163
Allium canadense. See wild onion
Allium cernuum. See nodding onion
Allium tricoccum. See ramps
Allium vineale. See wild garlic
Ambrosia artemisiifolia. See ragweed
American wild plum (*Prunus americana*),
    148–152, *148*, *149*, 152
  almond-flavored extract from, 150
  feasting on, 150
  ID checklist, 153, *153*
  other species of, 151, *151*
  where and how to find, 152
Apocynum cannabinum. See dogbane
Arctium lappa, A. minus. See burdock
Artemisia vulgaris. See mugwort
Asclepias syriaca, A. speciosa. See
    milkweed
Atriplex hortensis. See orache

B

banana yucca (*Yucca baccata*), 166–69,
    166, *168*
  edible parts of, 167–68
  ID checklist, 169, *169*
  where and how to find, 169

Barbarea vulgaris. See wintercress
beach plums (*Prunus maritima*), 151, *151*
blackberries. See bramble berries
black cherries (*Prunus serotina*), 128
black locust (*Robinia pseudoacacia*),
    116–121
  edible parts of, 118
  identifying, 117, 120–21, *121*
  look-alike, 119, *119*
  thorns of, 117, *117*
  where and how to find, 120
black raspberries. See bramble berries
blanching wild foods, 228–29, *228*
bract leaf shape, 22, 22
bramble berries (*Rubus* species), 122–25,
    122
  feasting on, 123
  ID checklist, 125, *125*
  types and characteristics, 124, *124*
  where and how to find, 125
bud(s), 24
  bud break, 14
  dandelion, 32
  magnolia, 135, 136, *136*
  milkweed, 85, 86, 87, *87*
  sow thistle, 57, *57*
  wintercress, 220
burdock (*Arctium lappa, A. minus*), *172*,
    173–76, *173*, *174*
  edible parts of, 175, *175*
  harvesting, 174
  ID checklist, 176, *176*
  where and how to find, 176

C

D

E

F

flowers, 24, *24*. See also bud(s); *specific plant*
  Cream, Infusing, 240
  Soda, Naturally Fermented, 232–33
  Syrup, Flower, 234
  Vinegar, 235
freezing wild foods
  blanching and, 228–29, *229*
  without blanching, 230
fruits, 24, 25. See also *specific fruit*
  Fruit-Infused Spirits, 237
  Jelly, 238–39
  jelly bag and stand for, 224, *224*
  ripeness and, 25
  Spirits, Fruit-Infused, 237
  steam juicer for, 225, *225*
  Wine, 236

G

Galinsoga parviflora, G. quadriradiata.
  See quickweed
garlic. See wild garlic
garlic mustard, 16, 17, 18, 213
Gibbons, Euell, 195
Gleditsia triacanthos. See honey locust tree
ground elder (*Aegopodium podagraria*), 212, *212*

H

Haines, Arthur, 118
harvesting. See also *specific plant*
  tools for, 26–27, *26*, *27*
honey locust tree (*Gleditsia triacanthos*), 119, *119*
Hydrophyllum virginianum. See Virginia waterleaf

I

invasive plants
  berries as, 125
  burdock as, 174
  definition of, 15–16
  dock as, 35
  melilot as, 81
  multiflora rose as, 159, *159*
  pulling up, 18
  Siberian elm as, 49, 50
  whitetop mustard as, 111
  wild garlic as, 62
Iris pseudacorus. See yellow flag iris

J

Japanese knotweed (*Reynoutria japonica*), 202–5
  edible parts of, 204
  ID checklist, 205, *205*
  stems, 20, *20*
  where and how to find, 204
Jelly, 238–39
  jelly bag and stand for, 224, *224*

K

kitchen tools, 224–25, *224*, *225*
knotweed. See Japanese knotweed

L

lamb's quarters (*Chenopodium species*), *21*, *72*, 73–75
  edible parts of, 73–74
  ID checklist, 75, *75*
  where and how to find, 75
lanceolate leaf shape, 22, *22*
Laportea canadensis. See wood nettle
leaflet, compound leaf, 23, *23*
leaves, 21, *21*. See also *specific plant*
  shapes of, 22, *22*–23, *23*

INTERIOR PHOTOGRAPHY CREDITS

Interior photography by © Ellen Zachos

Additional photography by © A.Kolos/Shutterstock.com, 75 t.; © Aaron J Hill/
Shutterstock.com, 153 t.; © adina munteanu/Shutterstock.com, 132 b.r.; © Adrian Davies/
naturepl.com, 93 b.r.; © Agata Gładykowska/Alamy Stock Photo, 121 b.r.; © Al.geba/
Shutterstock.com, 133 t.; © Albina Bugarcheva/Shutterstock.com, 228; © Aldercy Carling/
Alamy Stock Photo, 121 l.; © Alexander Denisenko/Shutterstock.com, 151 t.; © alexmak7/
Shutterstock.com, 124 t.l.; © All Canada Photos/Alamy Stock Photo, 46; © Alter-ego/
Shutterstock.com, 124 t.r.; © Andrejs Marcenko/Shutterstock.com, 155; © Andrii
Zastrozhnov/iStock.com, 245; © Anna Gratys/Shutterstock.com, 76; © anna.q/
Shutterstock.com, 152; AnRo0002/CC0/Wikimedia Commons, 61; © Arterra Picture
Library/Alamy Stock Photo, 62 l.; © Artur Bociarski/Shutterstock.com, 71 b.l.; © Avalon.red/
Alamy Stock Photo, 137 t.l.; © B Christopher/Alamy Stock Photo, 194; © barmalini/
Shutterstock.com, 4, 206; © Beekeepx/Shutterstock.com, 164 l.; © Bhupinder Bagga/
Shutterstock.com, 58 b.; © Big Joe/Shutterstock.com, 148; © Bill Gorum/Alamy Stock
Photo, 169 t.r.; © blickwinkel/Alamy Stock Photo, 33 b., 69, 134, 156 t., 191 t.; © Brian &
Sophia Fuller/Alamy Stock Photo, 201, t.; © Bryan Reynolds/Alamy Stock Photo, 63 t., 89
t.r.; © CampSmoke/Shutterstock.com, 213; © Carmen Rieb/Shutterstock.com, 124 b.r.;
© chapin31/iStock.com, 129 t.l.; © Chocoholic/Stockimo/Alamy Stock Photo, 125 b.l.;
© Christian Hütter/Alamy Stock Photo, 172; © cmac2009/Shutterstock.com, 101 b.;
© Creaturart Images/Shutterstock.com, 111; © cynoclub/Shutterstock.com, 113 t.; © dadalia/
iStock.com, 34; © Danny Hummel/Shutterstock.com, 63 b.; © David Bokuchava/
Shutterstock.com, 212 l.; © David Jackson/Alamy Stock Photo, 186; © David Stuckel/Alamy
Stock Photo, 125 r.; © Deanna Laing/Shutterstock.com, 165 t.l.; © Denis Lyagin/
Shutterstock.com, 47 b.; © Derek Croucher/Alamy Stock Photo, 185; © Dmitry Potashkin/
iStock.com, 119 b.l.; © Doikanoy/Shutterstock.com, 28, 56 l.; © DUSAN ZIDAR/
Shutterstock.com, 31; © Early Spring/Shutterstock.com, 26 b.l.; © Eduard Kalinin/
Shutterstock.com, 53 l.; © Eileen Kumpf/Shutterstock.com, 97 b.r.; © EKramar/Shutterstock
.com, 36 t.; © Eleonora Scordo/Shutterstock.com, 97 t.r.; © Emilio100/Shutterstock.com,
91 l.; © Erik Agar/Shutterstock.com, 189 t.; © Fabian Junge/Shutterstock.com, 24 r.; © Film
Adventure/Shutterstock.com, 135; © Fir Mamat/Alamy Stock Photo, 143 r.; © FloralImages/
Alamy Stock Photo, 197 b.; © Florapix/Alamy Stock Photo, 98 l., 178; © florin28/123RF.com,
94; © Flower_Garden/Shutterstock.com, 56 t.r.; © ForestSeasons/Shutterstock.com, 147 b.;

© Formatoriginal/Shutterstock.com, 154; © FotoHelin/Shutterstock.com, 1; © Frank G Cornish/Shutterstock.com, 137 b.; © Frank Hecker/Alamy Stock Photo, 100 t., 196 b., 200; © Furiarossa/Shutterstock.com, 163; © Gaston Cerliani/Shutterstock.com, 80 r.; © george photo cm/Shutterstock.com, 137 t.r.; © Gerry Bishop/Shutterstock.com, 146, 173; © Grigorii Pisotsckii/Shutterstock.com, 43 t.; © guentermanaus/Shutterstock.com, 117, 205 b.; © H. Mark Weidman Photography/Alamy Stock Photo, 168; © Hanjo Hellmann/ Alamy Stock Photo, 143 l.; © hans engbers/Shutterstock.com, 53 b.r.; © Hans Stuessi/ Alamy Stock Photo, 100 b.; © Hans-Joachim Schneider/Alamy Stock Photo, 136; © Hem Stock/Shutterstock.com, 74, 66; © Hemis/Alamy Stock Photo, 209 l.; © IhorM/Shutterstock .com, 209 r.; © Image Professionals GmbH/GAP Photos, 106; © imageBROKER/Alamy Stock Photo, 221 b.r.; © Imladris/Shutterstock.com, 105 b.; © In Stock/iStock.com, 2; © INTREEGUE Photography/Shutterstock.com, 123; © Irene Fox/Shutterstock.com, 119 t.l.; © Irina Borsuchenko/Shutterstock.com, 50 l., 98 r.; © Irina Fuks/Shutterstock.com, 97 l.; © Isabelle OHara/Shutterstock.com, 151 b.l.; © Island Images/Alamy Stock Photo, 231; © Jacek Fulawka/Shutterstock.com, 26 b.r.; © jadhavvikas/Shutterstock.com, 50 r.; © Jalpa Malam/Alamy Stock Photo, 104 b.; © Jay Ondreicka/Shutterstock.com, 205 m.; © Jeff March/Alamy Stock Photo, 127; © John_P_Anderson/Shutterstock.com, 56 b.r.; © Jose B. Ruiz/naturepl.com, 77 r.; © juerginho/Shutterstock.com, 202; © Kalfa/Shutterstock.com, 183 r.; © Karel Bock/Shutterstock.com, 17, 210; © Karin Jaehne/Shutterstock.com, 101 t.; © Karl Zhong/Shutterstock.com, 131; © Kevin Knight/Alamy Stock Photo, 151 b.r.; © Kristyna Henkeova/Shutterstock.com, 182; © Lekali Studio/Shutterstock.com, 89 t.l.; © Linda Pitkin/ naturepl.com, 79 m., 103 b., 105 t.; © M. Schuppich/Shutterstock.com, 196 t.; © Manfred Ruckszio/Shutterstock.com, 32, 35, 42, 187 t.; © marco mayer/Shutterstock.com, 224 l.; © Marcus Harrison - plants/Alamy Stock Photo, 59; © Maren Winter/Shutterstock.com, 33 t.; © Marinodenisenko/Shutterstock.com, 147 m.r.; © Mariola Anna S/Shutterstock.com, 89 b.l.; Mars Vilaubi © Storey Publishing, LLC, 27 t.r., 125 t.l.; © Martin Fowler/Shutterstock .com, 54; © Mastering_Microstock/Shutterstock.com, 51; © Matauw/Shutterstock.com, 198; © Md Sojibul Islam/Alamy Stock Photo, 104 m.; © meunierd/Shutterstock.com, 84; © Michele M Vogel/Shutterstock.com, 85; © Mike Read/Alamy Stock Photo, 81; © mimohe/Shutterstock.com, 183 l.; © MIROFOSS/Shutterstock.com, 211; © Miyuki Satake/Alamy Stock Photo, 176; © moguramenbou/Shutterstock.com, 48; Nadiatalent/ CC BY-SA 4.0/Wikimedia Commons, 11; © Nadin76/Shutterstock.com, 165 b.l.; © Nahhana/Shutterstock.com, 118, 147 m.l.; © Napat Aor70/Shutterstock.com, 87 b.; © Natalia Alexandrova/Alamy Stock Photo, 108; © Natalka De/Shutterstock.com, 120, 159;

EXPAND YOUR FORAGING ADVENTURES
with These Storey Books

How to Forage for Mushrooms without Dying

by Frank Hyman

This straightforward handbook shows you exactly how to identify 29 common, edible, delicious mushrooms that grow in the wild. With expert Frank Hyman as your guide, you'll learn to confidently identify which mushrooms you can safely eat and which you should definitely avoid.

Backyard Foraging

by Ellen Zachos

Ideal for first-time foragers, this book shows you how to identify 70 edible weeds, flowers, mushrooms, and ornamental plants typically found in urban and suburban areas. Full-color photographs make identification easy, and expert information makes foraging as safe and simple as stepping outside.

The Wildcrafted Cocktail

by Ellen Zachos

It's easy and fun to make delicious, one-of-a-kind mixed drinks with common flowers, berries, roots, and leaves that you can find along roadsides or in your yard. Expert Ellen Zachos offers recipes for more than 50 garnishes, syrups, infusions, juices, and bitters that you can make from foraged ingredients and then use in 45 surprising and delightful cocktails.
